Network Services Management

IT Infrastructure Library

Colin Rudd, Ultracomp
Alan Shilling, CCTA

London: The Stationery Office

© Crown Copyright 1994 Published for the
CCTA under licence from the Controller of
Her Majesty's Stationery Office.

Applications for reproduction
should be made in writing to the Copyright
Unit, Her Majesty's Stationery Office,
St. Clements House, 2–16 Colegate, Norwich
NR3 1BQ

Third impression 1997

ISBN   0 11 330558 3

ISSN   0956–2591

For further information on CCTA products,
contact:

CCTA Library
Rosebery Court
St Andrews Business Park
Norwich NR7 0HS

This document has been produced using
procedures conforming to
BSI 5750 Part I: 1987; ISO 9001: 1987.

This is one of the books published in the IT
Infrastructure Library series.

Table of contents

1.	**Management summary**	1
1.1	Introduction	1
1.2	The problem	1
1.3	This module	2
1.4	The benefits of managing network services	2
2.	**Introduction**	5
2.1	Purpose of this module	5
2.2	Target readership	6
2.3	Scope	6
2.4	Related guidance	7
2.5	Standards	9
3.	**Planning for Network Services Management**	13
3.0	Introduction	13
3.0.1	Classification of networks	13
3.0.2	Centralization vs de-centralization of management	18
3.0.3	Overview of network planning	19
3.0.4	Relationships with major management and planning activities	21
3.0.5	The four distinct disciplines	23
3.0.6	Organizational structure	24
3.0.7	Managing an outsourced network	25
3.0.8	Different rôles of NSM	26
3.0.9	The NSM 7-layer model	27
3.1	Procedures	33
3.1.1	Initiate project	33
3.1.2	Agree objectives and terms of reference of NSM	34
3.1.3	Objectives	34
3.1.4	Terms of reference	35
3.1.5	Initiate feasibility study	43
3.1.6	Obtain approval	47
3.1.7	Produce project plan	47
3.1.8	Plan operational responsibilities and procedures	48
3.1.9	Select support tools	56
3.1.10	Plan staff training	56

3.1.11	Select/design accommodation and environment	57
3.1.12	Plan reviews and audits	58
3.1.13	Review implementation plan	58
3.2	Dependencies	58
3.3	People	59
3.3.1	Duties and qualifications	59
3.3.2	Training	61
3.3.3	Other personnel	62
3.4	Timing	63

4. Implementation — 65

4.1	Implementation procedures	65
4.1.1	Installation and testing of support tools	65
4.1.2	Training	65
4.1.3	Publicize implementation	65
4.1.4	Populate the NDB	66
4.1.5	Finalize reports	66
4.1.6	Conduct on-going publicity campaign	66
4.2	Dependencies	66
4.3	People	67
4.4	Timing	67

5. Post-implementation and audit — 69

5.1	Procedures	69
5.1.1	Project evaluation review	69
5.1.2	Post-implementation review	70
5.1.3	Ongoing operation and review	71
5.1.4	Reviewing for efficiency and effectiveness	71
5.1.5	Auditing for compliance	73
5.2	Dependencies	73
5.3	People	74
5.4	Timing	75

6. Benefits, costs and possible problems — 77

6.1	Benefits	77
6.1.1	Benefits to the business	77
6.1.2	Benefits to IT Services	77

6.2	Costs	78
6.3	Possible problems	78
7.	**Tools**	**81**
7.1	Introduction	81
7.2	Network management systems (NMSs)	82
7.2.1	The proprietary approach to NMSs	82
7.2.2	The non-proprietary approach to NMSs	83
7.2.3	The integrated approach to NMSs	86
7.3	Tool requirement	88
7.3.1	Functional requirements	88
7.3.2	Tool categories	91
7.3.3	NSM requirements for categories of tool	106
7.4	Tool selection	106
7.5	Interface requirements	107
7.6	Current tools	107
7.7	Advantages and pitfalls	108
7.8	Summary	109
8.	**Bibliography**	**111**
8.1	References	111

Annexes

A.	**Glossary of terms**	**A1**
B.	**Job descriptions and qualifications of Network Services staff**	**B1**
B.1	Network Services Manager	B1
B.2	Network Services Planner	B3
B.3	Network Services Administrator	B5
B.4	Network Services Controller	B7
B.5	Network Services Project Controller	B9
C.	**Guidelines for reviewing current networks**	**C1**

D.	**Guidelines for a reference site visit**	D1
E.	**Network Services Management tools**	E1
F.	**Network management standards - future directions**	F1
F.1	Introduction	F1
F.2	Network management systems	F1
F.3	Network management standards	F2
G.	**Planning and implementing network services**	G1
G.1	Introduction	G1
G.2	Appoint team	G1
G.3	Requirements analysis	G2
G.4	Gap analysis	G3
G.5	Conduct outline sizing exercise	G3
G.6	Prepare and validate statement of requirements	G4
G.7	Conduct initial costing exercise	G5
G.8	Project plan	G6
G.9	Design network	G6
G.11	Integration with existing systems	G15
G.12	Costs	G15
G.13	Evaluation of options	G16
G.14	Finalize design	G16
G.15	Plan network implementation/enhancement	G17
H.	**Data network services**	H1
I.	**Voice network services**	I1

Foreword

Welcome to the IT Infrastructure Library module on **Network Services Management.**

In their respective areas the IT Infrastructure Library publications complement and provide more detail than the IS Guides.

The ethos behind the development of the IT Infrastructure Library is the recognition that organizations are becoming increasingly dependent on IT in order to satisfy their corporate aims and meet their business needs. This growing dependency leads to growing requirement for quality IT services. In this context quality means 'matched to business needs and user requirements as these evolve'.

This module is one of a series of codes of practice intended to facilitate the quality management of IT services and of the IT Infrastructure. (By IT Infrastructure, we mean organizations' computers and networks - hardware, software and computer related communications, upon which application systems and IT services are built and run). The codes of practice will assist organizations to provide quality IT services in the face of skill shortages, system complexity, rapid change, growing user expectations, current and future user requirements.

Underpinning the IT Infrastructure is the Environmental Infrastructure upon which it is built. Environmental topics are covered in separate sets of guides within the IT Infrastructure Library.

IT service management is a complex subject which for presentational and practical reasons has been broken down within the IT Infrastructure Library into a series of modules. A complete list of current and planned modules is available from the CCTA IT Infrastructure Management Services at the address given at the back of this module.

IT Infrastructure Library
Network Services Management

The structure of the module is, in essence:

* a **Management summary** aimed at senior managers (Directors of IT and above, typically down to Civil Service Grade 5), senior IT staff and, in some cases, users or office managers (typically Civil Service Grades 5 to 7)

* the main body of the text, aimed at IT middle management (typically grades 7 to HEO)

* technical detail in Annexes.

The module gives the main **guidance** in sections 3 to 5; explains the **benefits, costs and possible problems** in section 6, which may be of interest to senior staff; and provides information on **tools** (requirements and examples of real-life availability) in section 7.

CCTA is working with the IT industry to foster the development of software tools to underpin the guidance contained within the codes of practice (ie to make adherence to the module more practicable), and ultimately to automate functions.

If you have any comments on this or other modules, do please let us know. A **Comments sheet** is provided with every module. Alternatively you may wish to contact us directly using the reference point given in **Further information**.

Thank you. We hope you find this module useful.

Acknowledgement

The assistance of the following contributors is gratefully acknowledged:

Reviewers of the IT Infrastructure Management Forum (ITIMF)

Staff of Ultracomp Ltd.

Section 1
Management summary

1. Management summary

1.1 Introduction

The information highway — One of the most significant developments in IT has been the rapid growth in the number of computer terminals (and the concomitant supporting network infrastructures) both in the public and private sectors. This enormous growth is based on the need to automate costly, labour intensive processes (such as typing documents to be sent by post) and management's requirement to receive and manipulate information. It has brought to the forefront the need to provide a facility to manipulate information electronically and transport it around the organization. This transportation is achieved by means of telecommunications networks - the *information highway* of automated Information Systems.

1.2 The problem

Evolution — The technologies for handling different types of information (voice, data, video, facsimile etc) have evolved at different rates, leading to procurement of separate equipment to handle the different information transmissions. Often the management focus for the operation of each service rests with disparate parts of the organization (IT and non-IT) as different equipment is installed.

New technologies — The development of digital switching and transmission techniques now offers opportunities to combine voice, data and other services over common networks and create financial savings. New services (video conferencing, for example) are also possible.

The local network explosion — Many organizations have experienced a rapid, and ill-managed, growth in local area networks (LANs). These LANs often serve particular functional areas, but, through lack of a corporate strategy, are difficult to integrate and control. This limits the contribution that they can make to corporate business needs.

Security — The increasing dependency of organizations on complex interconnected networks highlights the need to protect the confidentiality, integrity and availability of networks, the services they provide and the information that they handle.

Managing it all — Managing a telecommunications network has rapidly become a major task because of:

* the differing rates of evolution of current technologies

* emerging technologies
* the need to coordinate the myriad of ad-hoc local networks and stand-alone PCs installed in many organizations.

1.3 This module

The Network Services Management module of the IT Infrastructure Library defines the management procedures necessary to provide a quality network service, either direct to end-users (typically a telephone network) or as a component part of a larger system (typically an IT system).

The module also examines the planning and design issues necessary to allow coherent network growth. This module takes the view that customers require a service and that the means of providing the service is of little consequence provided business needs are met, at a cost that the business can afford. In the past, Service Level Agreements (SLAs) have been created without due regard to the effects of networks on customer services. It is a common occurrence to see, for example, a transaction response time defined as 'within two seconds (excluding network transmission time)': the value of fully understanding the impact of network services design and management on customer services cannot be over-estimated and this module promotes the view that network services should be managed in the same way as any other service, ie the customer comes first. IT Services are responsible for the entire service, which includes the network, and must not abdicate responsibility for managing the network by including let-out clauses such as that quoted above.

In effect, Network Services Management describes the application of IT Service Management disciplines, such as Capacity, Change and Configuration Management, to the management of network services.

1.4 The benefits of managing network services

Benefits to the business

The business benefit stemming from effective Network Services Management is the reliable and consistent matching of network services to user needs (ie **service quality**), which, in turn, contributes to the overall success of the organization's business through higher productivity. This benefit is achieved through:

* increased service availability to users
* capacity matched to users' requirements

Section 1
Management summary

* less adverse impact of changes on the quality of IT services, because changes are carefully controlled
* more efficient handling of problems
* lower costs of IT service provision (through the benefits to IT Services)
* reducing the risk of network failure and minimizing the effect of such failure.

Benefits to IT Services   Network Services Management helps IT Services become more efficient and effective by:

* managing changes to network hardware and software - reducing the resources needed to cope with the adverse effects of changes
* managing problems - monitoring network service levels enables trends and problems to be identified quickly and dealt with, reducing the resources required to handle problems; analysing the cause of problems helps to reduce the number of problems
* anticipating problems - potential performance, capacity, and availability problems can be anticipated, and corrective action instigated to prevent a crisis
* helping the IT directorate to understand their network infrastructures, leading to more informed decisions
* increased productivity of key IT personnel (less fire-fighting)
* reducing risk of not meeting commitments
* identifying new technology which could save costs and/or improve service levels
* planning expansions and upgrades - by maintaining a close match between demand and capacity the organization makes efficient use of resources.

The IT Infrastructure Library
Network Services Management

2. Introduction

There are several underlying reasons why the effective, proactive, management of telecommunications networks is becoming more important:

* dependency - organizations are increasingly dependent on IT services of which major components are IT systems and network services

* complexity - networks are becoming larger and more complex

* flexibility - changing business requirements mean that users are demanding new services, to be provided by the existing infrastructure

* provision of quality IT services is dependent on networks - specifically for improved performance, availability and functionality from networked information systems

* customer satisfaction - customers have become less tolerant of poor network services owing to the severe impact that network failures have on mainstream business functions

* increased visibility of 'front office' systems.

Network technology is evolving rapidly, with more complex and sophisticated systems and services being introduced in shorter time intervals. The range of options now available, coupled with the lack of comprehensive standards represents a daunting challenge to the network services planner.

It is the Network Services Manager's responsibility to ensure that these issues are adequately addressed, and that the existing network infrastructure of systems, services, people and procedures is managed effectively.

2.1 Purpose of this module

The purpose of this module is to give guidance on the planning and on-going management of networks and network services. Good planning, administration and control are key to ensuring that network services provide the information highway necessary to implement the effective Information Systems upon which organizations depend to meet business needs cost-effectively.

2.2 Target readership

This document is primarily aimed at:

* Directors of IT (management summary only)
* Network Services Managers and their staff
* Network Services Management implementation project leaders and team members
* IT Service Managers and their staff
* IT Project Managers.

It will also be of interest to managers of voice communications and the Service Control Team (SCT) where network services are outsourced.

Knowledgeable business managers may find sections 1, 2, 3.0.1 to 3.0.7 and sections 5 and 6 of interest.

Readers of this module should be aiming to adopt the practices described in the module, *on a scale appropriate to the size and complexity of the services to be managed.*

2.3 Scope

Network Services Management (NSM)

The module gives guidance on the planning, implementation and on-going operation of the Network Services Management (NSM) function.

The guidance in the module splits the responsibilities of NSM into four major parts:

* **Network Services Planning (NSP)**, which encompasses the strategic and tactical planning processes undertaken prior to implementing or enhancing a network service

* **Network Services Administration (NSA)**, which includes the tactical planning and implementation of network equipment and second line support for the NSC function

* **Network Services Control (NSC)**, which provides the day-to-day operation and control of the network and network services and provides the interface between the Help Desk and NSA

* **Network Services Project Control (NSPC)**, providing the project management and control of major new networks or network enhancement projects.

Section 2
Introduction

Guidance is also given on the post-implementation procedures required to review the management of network services and on how to conduct regular effectiveness and efficiency reviews.

What isn't covered

It is important to appreciate that managing network services is a microcosm of managing the IT infrastructure. Most of the procedures and practices required to manage the IT infrastructure effectively need to be applied to the network services area. Therefore extensive reference is made in this module to other modules of the IT Infrastructure Library for details on topics such as Change Management, Problem Management and Capacity Management, where these are considered appropriate.

Networks

The module deals with the issues involved in the planning and design of both voice and data telecommunications networks (in annex G), but it does not cover technical issues in any detail, although this is sometimes unavoidable. The issues it addresses are equally applicable to local and wide area networks. It does not attempt to deal with the management of remote computer systems or of distributed IT services - see the **Management of Local Processors and Terminals** module for guidance on these issues.

Standards and new types of service

The current status, relevance, and issues arising from standards such as Open Systems Interconnection (OSI) and new types of service such as Integrated Services Digital Networks (ISDNs) are discussed, but technology based topics are not dealt with in detail.

2.4 Related guidance

This module is one of a series that constitutes the CCTA **IT Infrastructure Library**. Although the module can be read in isolation, **given the nature of the guidance in this particular module, it is strongly recommended that it is used in conjunction with other modules**. The following modules are of particular significance.

Availability Management

Network Services Managers must plan and monitor the availability for all aspects of network services and ensure that maintenance, repair and recovery activities are carried out in a timely manner. Networks should be planned to maximize availability of the service and minimize the impact of failure, by designing in resilience and redundancy.

Cable Infrastructure Strategy

Network planning and cable infrastructure are inextricably linked. This module explains why a cable infrastructure is a strategic issue.

The IT Infrastructure Library
Network Services Management

Capacity Management	There must be sufficient network capacity to support the demands for new and improved IT services while allowing current service performance targets to be met. Annexes in the **Capacity Management** module describe how to match capacity and demand. Annex B.5 covers the monitoring of network performance. Annex C.2 covers performance management of networks. Annex C.3.2 covers the use of the Network Database. Annex E.5 covers network modelling. Annex H covers application sizing for distributed systems.
Change Management	The complexities and interworking associated with a network are such that the management of change is essential.
Computer Operations Management	It is necessary for the Network Services Manager and the Computer Operations Manager to cooperate fully in running the organization's networks and computers.
Configuration Management	All the assets of an IT service, including communications networks, network services, and the dependencies between them, need to be controlled and managed; the network may be used as a vehicle for automated configuration audits and potentially as a means to implement a distributed configuration management database (CMDB).
Contingency Planning	Particularly important for networks because contingency generally has to be designed in; the option of a stand-by system is not usually feasible or cost effective, although alternative third-party suppliers, or individual elements, could be.
Cost Management for IT Services	Keeping within budget is of concern to all IT managers including the Network Services Manager.
Help Desk	It is necessary to provide a well managed single point of contact for all users of network services.
Management of Local Processors and Terminals	The division of responsibilities between the Management of Local Processors and Terminals (MLPT) and Network Services Management functions must be clearly defined because of the obvious overlap between IT resources management requirements which may be considered to be either network or local, depending on the viewpoint chosen.
Managing Facilities Management	A number of external network service providers offer a range of 'managed network services' and the advice contained in this module is relevant if use is made of external service providers, other than for the provision of simple network elements.
Managing Supplier Relationships	An important issue for the management of network services where it is common for the components and services to be provided by a number of different suppliers.

Section 2
Introduction

Problem Management	The efficient and effective resolution of incidents and problems is as essential in a networked environment as in a centralized system.
Quality Management for IT Services	A quality management system for IT Services encompasses network services management (if networks are in existence) and will require the specification of the procedures described in this module.
Service Level Management	The Network Services Manager must contribute and agree to the contract terms contained in SLAs; the Network Services Manager is responsible for the quality of service specified in the SLAs in terms of the underpinning agreements for network services, particularly availability.
Software Control and Distribution	The network may be used as a vehicle for the more effective and efficient distribution of software to physically dispersed hardware; it also presents the opportunity for fully automated distribution of software and other electronic information.
	Network software (ie that used in telecommunications devices) should be brought under the control of the Software Control and Distribution (SC&D) function.
Specification and Management of a Cable Infrastructure	The specification of a cable infrastructure is effectively low level network design and will influence the design of the rest of the network. This module is essential reading for Network Services Planners.
Third Party and Single Source Maintenance	This module gives guidance, for those organizations considering Third Party or Single Source Maintenance contracts, on specifying a Statement of Service Requirements (previously called Operational Requirements) for maintenance, selecting contractors and managing the ongoing relationship with the maintainer. This guidance is generic and therefore equally applicable to Third Party and Single Source Maintenance of networks.
Unattended Operations	Various categories of unattended operation require at least a simple network in order to be feasible. For systems where many sites are unattended and monitored centrally, the network is the essential feature which makes unattended operation both feasible and cost effective.

2.5 Standards

The following standards are applicable to Network Services Management.

CRAMM

The CCTA Risk Analysis and Management Method is a complete package which provides a structured and consistent basis to identify and justify all the protective measures necessary to ensure the security of both current and future IT systems used for processing (and handling the transmission of) sensitive data.

UK GOSIP

UK GOSIP is a set of guidance designed to simplify the use of the International Open Systems Interconnection (OSI) standards for people who are involved in the planning and purchase of communications-based computer equipment. UK GOSIP has been developed by CCTA with the support of government departments and information technology (IT) suppliers.

EPHOS

To reinforce its work on GOSIP, CCTA has been active with its counterparts in France and Germany, via the Public Procurement Group (PPG), collaborating on a European Commission funded project to harmonize the Open Systems procurement guidance throughout Europe.

The technical content of the three areas which comprise the European Handbook for Open Systems (EPHOS) is identical to that used in the same sections of GOSIP. GOSIP users should have every confidence that their current and future directions and investments are safeguarded.

In the short term, CCTA plans to use the results from the EPHOS project as input to the continuous programme of improvement to UK GOSIP, therefore, in the short term, organizations should use GOSIP advice where appropriate. However, in the longer term CCTA will look to the EPHOS project to provide the major source of procurement guidance for purchasers of Information Systems based on Open Systems standards.

PRINCE

The planning and implementation of a Network Services Management function should normally be executed as a formally defined and managed project. Projects in Controlled Environments (PRINCE) is the preferred Government method for project management.

ISO 9001/EN29001/BS5750 Part 1 - Quality Management and Quality Assurance Standards

The IT Infrastructure Library modules are designed to assist adherents, for example organizations' IT Directorates, to obtain third-party quality certification to ISO 9001. Such third parties should be accredited by the NACCB, the National Accreditation Council for Certification Bodies.

Section 2
Introduction

UK ITSEC

The UK IT Security Evaluation and Certification Scheme is designed to meet the needs of industry, commerce and government departments, for the security evaluation and certification of IT products (whether hardware or software) and systems; and to provide a basis for the international mutual recognition of evaluation results and certificates.

The scheme is operated jointly by the Department of Trade and Industry (DTI) and the Communications-Electronics Security Group (CESG).

The DTI and CESG are producing a series of UK Scheme Publications - UKSPs. Further information on the scheme can be found in the first of the series, UKSP 01 - Description of the Scheme.

Further details may be obtained from:

> Head of the Certification Body
> UK IT Security Evaluation & Certification Scheme
> Room 2/0805
> Fiddlers Green Lane
> Cheltenham
> Gloucestershire
> GL52 5AJ.

Regulatory requirements

The deregulation and liberalization of the UK telecommunications environment allows significant freedom of choice for the user of telecommunications systems and services.

However, this new environment creates new responsibilities for system and service providers and users. A number of statutory requirements must be met when providing and using telecommunications systems, services and networks.

In particular, network planners and designers must be familiar with the requirements of the Office of Telecommunications (OFTEL), the British Standards Institute (BSI), and the British Approvals Board for Telecommunications (BABT).

Attention must also be paid to the restrictions and guidelines detailed in the:

* Network Code of Practice
* Oftel Requirements and Approvals Issues
* Health and Safety at Work etc Act

* British Standards

    - EN 41 003:1991- Particular safety requirements for equipment to be connected to telecommunication networks (as BS EN 41 003:1993, superseded BS 6301:1989 on 15 September 1993 and became the designated standard)

    - BS 6305:1982 - Specification for general requirements for apparatus for connection to the British Telecommunications public switched telephone networks (cited in 1984 Act)

    - BS 6305:1992 - Specification for general requirements for apparatus for connection to public switched telephone networks (presented for designation and when accepted would replace the 1982 version.)

    - NET 4:1988 - Access to PSTN (simple terminals only) (to supersede BS 6305 after April 1994)

    - BS6789 - Apparatus with one or more particular functions for connection to public switched telephone networks run by certain public telecommunications operators (a multipart standard; the various parts have been presented for designation under the 1984 Act)

    - BS6328 - Apparatus for connection to private circuits run by certain public telecommunication operators (a multipart standard; the various parts have been presented for designation under the 1984 Act)

    - BS6450 - Private branch exchanges for connection to public switched telephone networks run by certain public telecommunications operators (a multipart standard;some parts have been presented for designation under the 1984 Act)

    - BS 6701 - Code of practice for installation of apparatus intended for connection to certain telecommunication systems (not required by 1984 Act).

It is also important that due account is taken of other standards, both non-proprietary, (eg those administered by ITU/TS (formerly CCITT), CCTA, CEPT, ISO, ETSI, ANSI, ECMA, EIA, IEE and the Network Management Forum) and proprietary, (eg IBM NetView, DEC, ICL). If the organization has a stated policy in these areas, it must be communicated to the project teams involved, and will probably be laid out in the organization's IS Strategy.

Section 3
Planning for Network Services Management

3. Planning for Network Services Management

This section describes the planning which is required for the creation or improvement of a Network Services Management (NSM) function.

3.0 Introduction

3.0.1 Classification of networks

Networks fall into three general classifications : voice, data and hybrid. Each of these types is considered in the following sections, although the distinction between voice and data networks is rapidly disappearing.

3.0.1.1 Voice systems

Voice networks have been viewed as less complex, and therefore easier to manage than data networks because:

* the technology was, in general, well established

* voice communications are generally conducted via a path which, following an initial connection, is fixed for the duration of a call

* voice communications are not so sensitive to transmission errors

* users' expectations are limited.

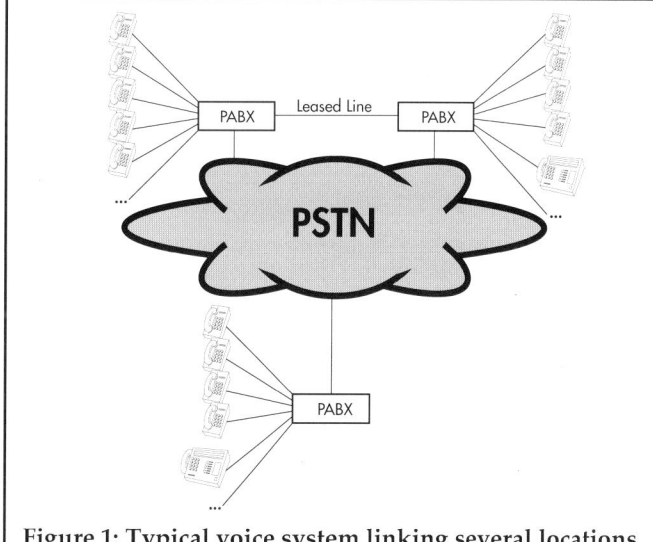

Figure 1: Typical voice system linking several locations and giving access to the public network

However, because the legacy of voice networks have been designed for voice traffic, that is:

* point-to-point, a circuit (or channel) is established before any transmission can be started, obviating any need for destination addresses on traffic

* lines are often analogue (particularly local lines), and therefore more prone to distortion, although this situation is changing

* local lines are of limited capacity

* transmission errors are not detected or corrected

they are inherently less suitable than data networks for carrying data traffic.

3.0.1.2 Data systems

Data networks tend to be more complex, and therefore more difficult to manage than voice networks because:

* the technology is not particularly well established and is changing rapidly

* routeing is usually dynamic

* cost effective communications require sharing of channels

* detection and correction of transmission errors is an important feature (although this may be done by applications software).

A network of computers or a computer network?

The management of data networks is governed by the context in which they operate. In order to simplify matters, within this module IT systems are classified as either:

* centralized

or

* de-centralized

although most networks will be some sort of hybrid.

Note: the term 'distributed system' has deliberately not been used because one strict definition of a distributed system is a de-centralized system which has a network-wide operating system that allows all of the computing resources on the network to be treated as one whole. The term 'distributed system' is often used loosely, without any qualification as to what the 'system' is!

Section 3
Planning for Network Services Management

Centralized data systems — Centralized data systems (see figure 2) are IT systems in which most of the services provided come from a central system (or *host*) such as a mainframe or minicomputer. In this case, the terminals have limited intelligence, the network plays a secondary rôle to the central processing facility, and the performance and capacity requirements of the network will strongly relate to the services provided by the central processing node.

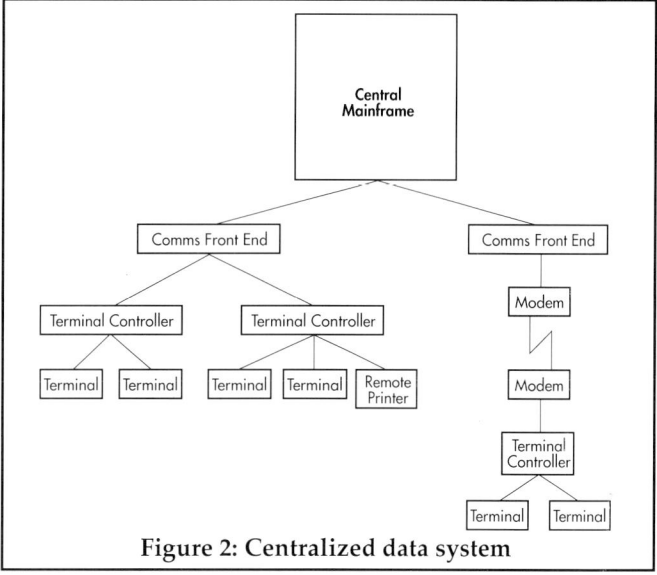

Figure 2: Centralized data system

Centralized systems are characterized by each primary service (such as a business application) being provided from one particular source. The management of the services is also provided centrally.

De-centralized data systems — De-centralized data systems (see figure 3) are IT systems (such as networks of PCs and file/print servers) in which a substantial amount of the services is provided by systems spread across the network. Large de-centralized systems may contain elements which can themselves be considered as centralized systems. In all de-centralized systems the communications network plays a more important rôle in the provision of at least some (and probably most) of the services, the capacity and performance is not easy to predict and will not be largely related to the services provided by any one processing node.

The network can play an important rôle in the management of the non-communications elements of de-centralized systems. It facilitates the efficient monitoring and control of computer systems and other devices connected to the network.

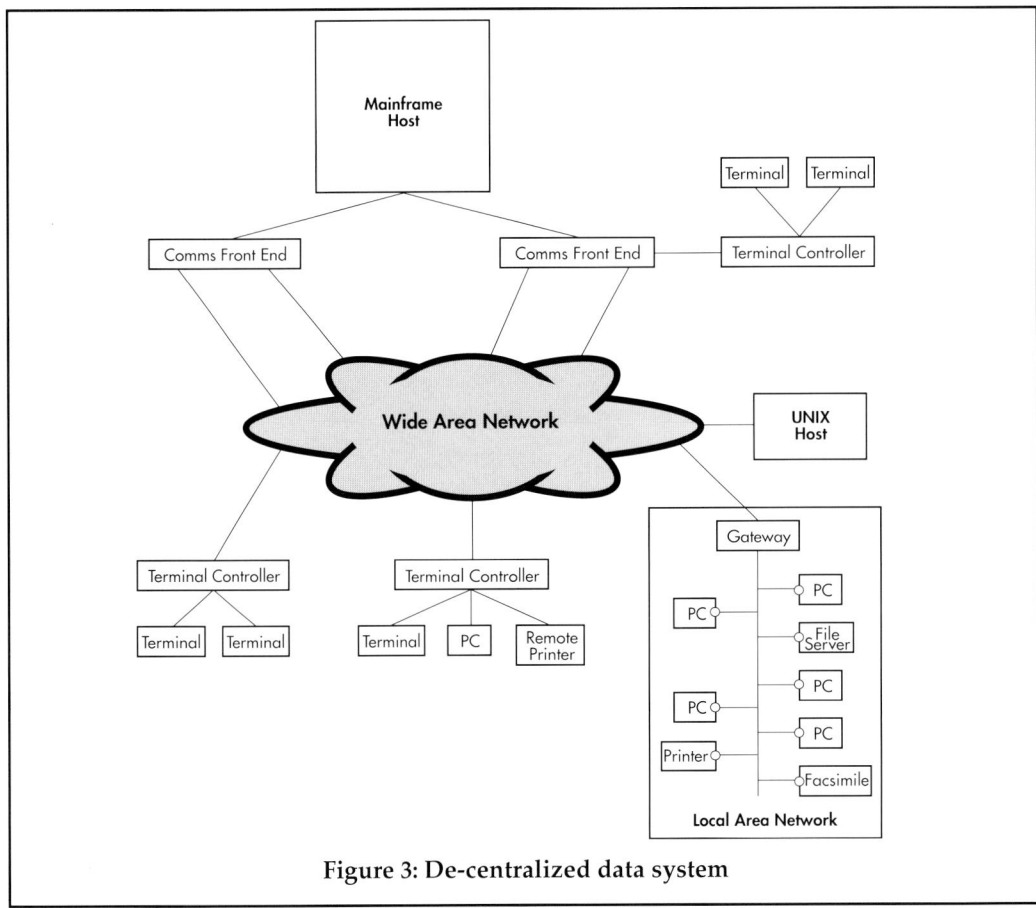

Figure 3: De-centralized data system

De-centralized systems are characterized by each service (such as a business application) being provided by component services from a number of different sources.

The management of services will be partially distributed but some central coordination will be necessary, particularly for configuration and change management.

3.0.1.3 Hybrid systems

Hybrid systems (see figure 4) share some or many components, such as a PABX which handles both voice and data transmissions. Hybrid systems may integrate voice, data, possibly video, and other media on a single, digital, transport system, with inherently greater transmission speed and capacity and more efficient use of the transport mechanism.

Section 3
Planning for Network Services Management

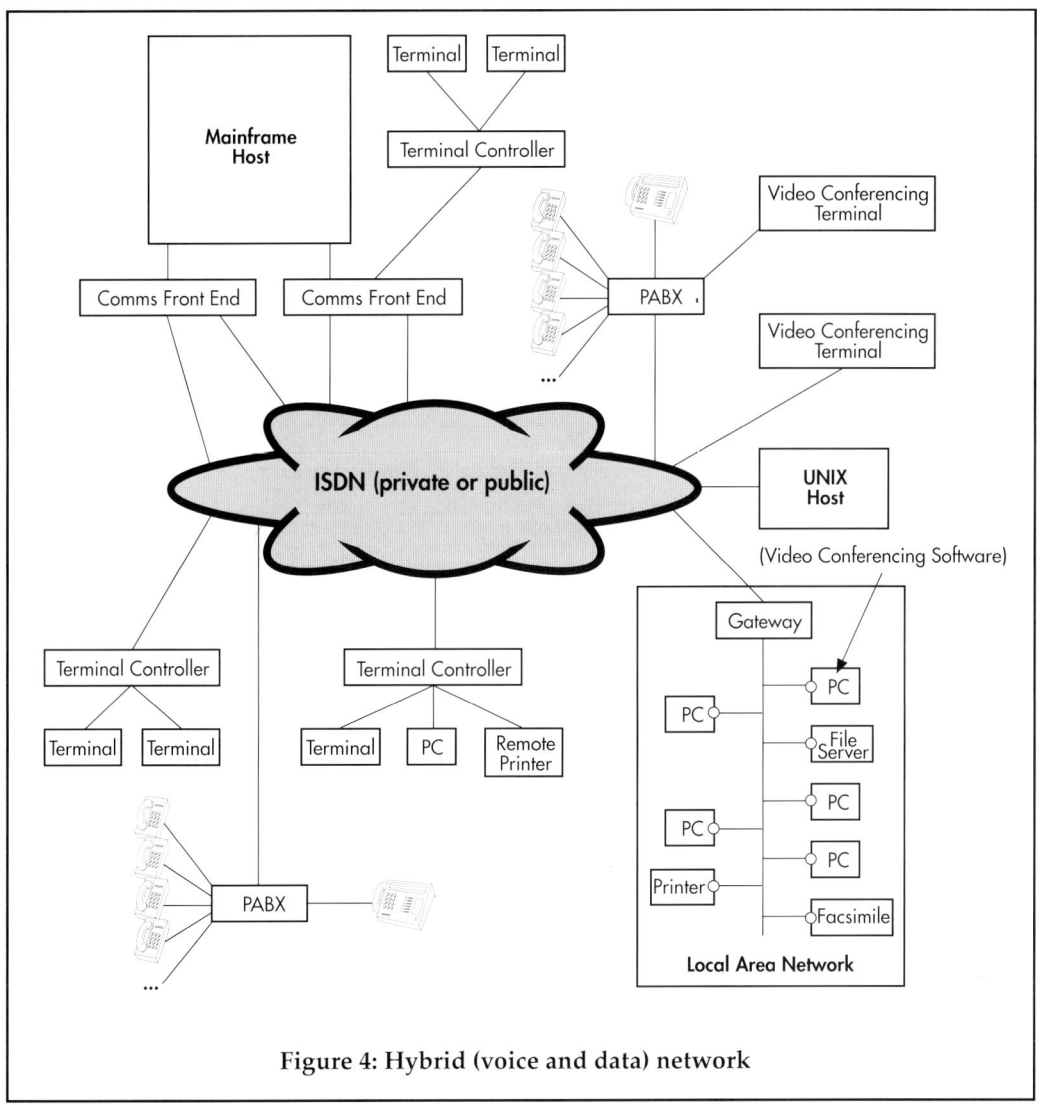

Figure 4: Hybrid (voice and data) network

Although it is currently possible to do this using services such as Integrated Services Digital Networks (ISDN), or through a private or leased link, use of such services may be limited by a legacy of analogue devices which need special hardware to be connected to digital links, and are constrained by the speed of the analogue connection. Current video conferencing facilities do however make use of ISDN. Total integration, for instance sending voice and video reliably from a video conferencing device to a desktop PC, through a typical (eg 10 Mbits/sec Ethernet)

LAN, is often a desirable rather than feasible option due to the performance constraints. Higher speed LANs offer a solution, at a cost, to this limitation.

3.0.2 Centralization vs de-centralization of management

The issue of centralizing or de-centralizing the control and support functions and staff can be decided on the basis of a range of considerations, including:

* the relative cost of running a centralized function versus that of running a dispersed function

* organizational policy

* the availability and efficient use of skilled staff

* the availability and efficient use of suitable accommodation

* the reliability of the network components

* the types of technology involved - if the technology is different at different locations, it may be sensible to retain some specialist functions at each location

* the characteristics of the user population - certain parts of the network may require more support than others

* the power of the network management tools - the tools may facilitate centralized control

* whether there are other support functions at dispersed sites (such as computer operations or local systems administrators).

In many cases, organizational policy takes precedence and may be the most difficult to change.

In general a centralized management strategy is beneficial and can have significant cost benefits associated with it. However, a minimum of two centres (but not necessarily with duplicate staff!) may be required for resilience and contingency purposes.

Given the complex and diverse nature of networks, it is advantageous to have a single point for specialist network support. This provides a focus for other parts of the IT services organization requiring technical support from NSM. This single point for specialist network support is the responsibility of the Network Services Administration (NSA) function and will have a thorough knowledge of the range of network services used.

Section 3
Planning for Network Services Management

3.0.3 Overview of network planning

The major objective of Network Services Management is to provide a network that facilitates provision of services to meet Service Level Agreements, both now and in the future. Network planning is a crucial aspect of fulfilling this objective. The Network Plan is the blueprint which helps to ensure that such a network will be provided. The Network Plan should be developed and maintained to satisfy the demands for new and modified network services based on the business requirements and the Business Strategy. This plan should contain details of both the networking strategy and the telecommunications strategy of the organization. This means that it should cover all elements of data, voice, image etc and integrated services and should therefore provide a comprehensive strategy for all the communications requirements of the whole organization. The plan should be all embracing and cover, where appropriate:

* backbone networks
* voice networks
* local area networks (LANs)
* wide area networks (WANs)
* metropolitan area networks (MANs)
* integrated services, such as ISDN
* network gateways
* cabling
* video
* imaging
* third party networks (PTTs and VANs)
* PCs and terminals (in conjunction with the Management of Local Processors and Terminals function)
* network servers and services (eg File, Print, Electronic mail and Fax servers)
* network management systems.

This plan should be regularly reviewed and refined in step with the needs of the business and the Business Strategy. A more detailed description of the contents of the Network Plan can be found in section 3.1.8.1.

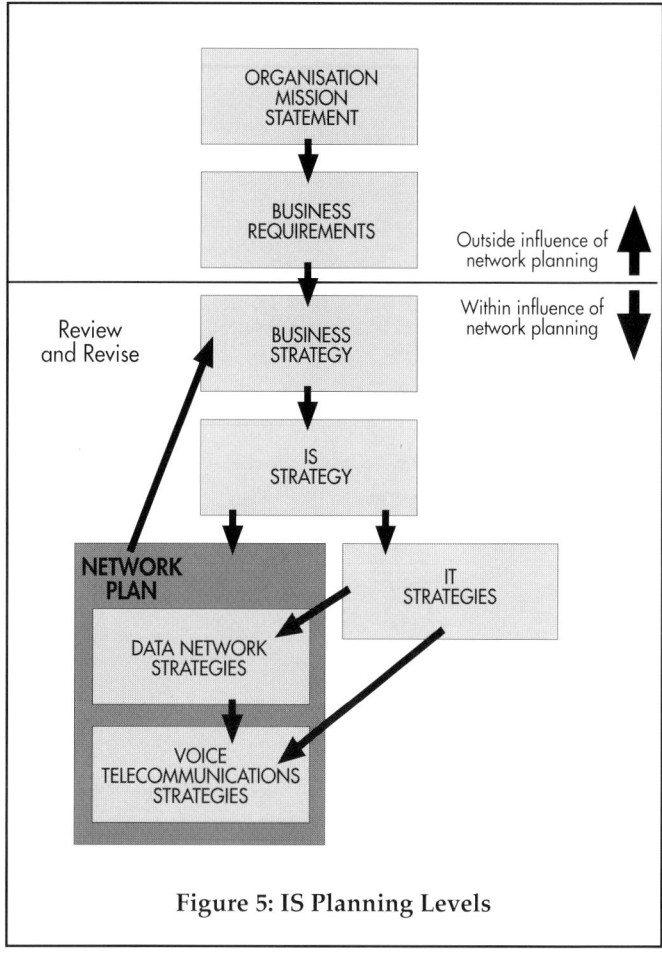

Figure 5: IS Planning Levels

Figure 5 illustrates the levels of planning for Information Systems, starting with the business requirements and the business strategy. This sets out the business managers' view of their demand for IS. At the higher levels (outside the scope of this module), business strategies are studied so that IS strategies and plans are designed to meet the data and voice network requirements of the business.

Notice that, as a side-effect of preparing a network plan, opportunities (eg due to technological developments) for business benefits may be identified and fed back into the development of the business strategy.

Section 3
Planning for Network Services Management

3.0.4 Relationships with major management and planning activities

The planning of Network Services should be carried out as part of an overall IT Planning process because:

* if network services are planned on a project by project, and/or voice and data separately, basis, the result is often many diverse types of networks being implemented which do not easily work together

* the installation of multiple and incompatible technologies in different functional areas of an organization inhibits the integration and effectiveness of cross-functional applications

* otherwise there is a lack of agreed standards and conformant products for open systems operation and management

* the economic savings of distributed computing architectures are most noticeable when considered across the organization

* the development of new technologies and services, such as multimedia, document image processing and electronic trading, present new business opportunities and integration challenges

* if networks are planned and developed centrally, sharing of links, equipment and resources can lead to significant savings, thereby simplifying the whole process of network cost justification

* availability, capacity, contingency and security requirements can then be met for the whole organization or business.

The programmes of work identified in the business strategy are refined into programmes of specific projects at the next level (programme planning). Changes to the supporting IT infrastructure may be managed and planned at this level (IT Infrastructure Planning).

Programme Management is the management of a set of related projects to deliver a business benefit which could not be achieved if the projects were managed as discrete items. Individual programmes are identified from the IS Strategy. Infrastructure Planning (or IT Infrastructure Planning) may be concerned with integrating the IT requirements of a number of programmes or it may be concerned with implementing an IT Strategy.

The IT Infrastructure Library
Network Services Management

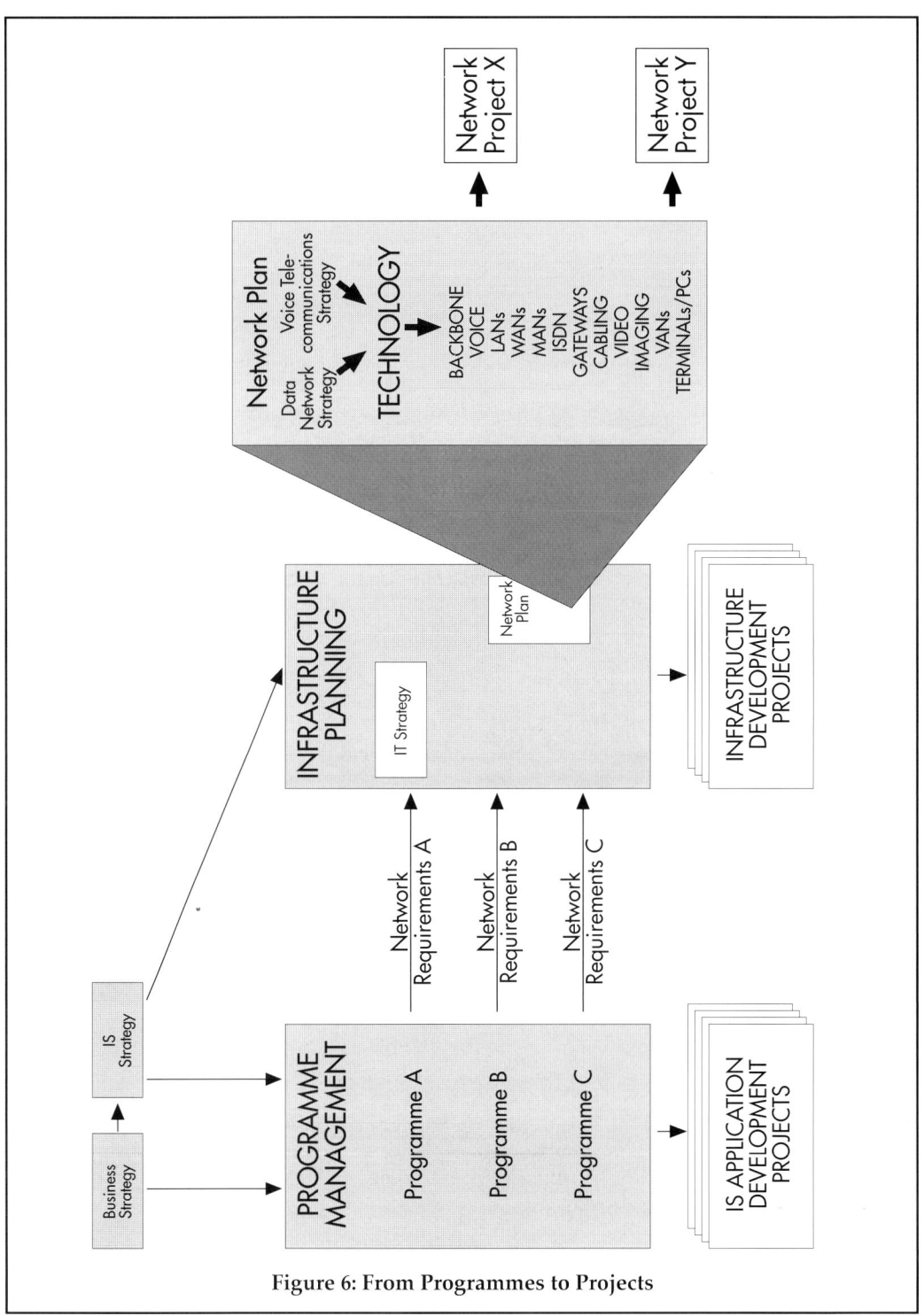

Figure 6: From Programmes to Projects

Section 3
Planning for Network Services Management

At the next level, the requirement for IT is turned into more detailed and realizable plans of action.

Individual projects and studies are shown at the lowest level, together with the IT infrastructure activities of planning and controlling the computers and networks of an organization, upon which application systems are built and IT services are run. This situation is illustrated in Figure 6. For further details of IT Infrastructure Planning, see CCTA's **An Introduction to IT Infrastructure Planning.**

3.0.5 The four distinct disciplines

Network Services Management (NSM) is responsible for coordinating the activities of the four supporting disciplines of NSM and providing the interfaces to other senior IT Management, IT Service Management and Business Management. It should provide a central point of contact and control of both local and remote network services staff. There are four distinct, yet inter-related, disciplines.

Network Services Planning (NSP) is the function that develops and maintains the strategic Network Plan that will underpin the business strategy. It is logical therefore that the Network Plan should attempt to cover the same timescales, and be reviewed with the same frequency as the Business Plan.

Network Services Administration (NSA) is responsible for the tactical planning and implementation of network equipment and information analysis and reports, rather than the strategic planning of network services. It also provides reinforcement for network support to the Network Services Control function.

Network Services Control (NSC) is responsible for the provision of the day-to-day operation and support of the network and network services and provides the interface between the Help Desk staff and NSA staff.

Network Services Project Control (NSPC) provides the project management and control of major new networks or network enhancement projects. This function will not in many cases be staffed on a permanent basis, but will utilize secondees from other networking functions. It could also be subsumed as part of an overall systems project control function (ie for major new de-centralized or hybrid systems).

The logical NSM structure is illustrated in Figure 7 overleaf.

The IT Infrastructure Library
Network Services Management

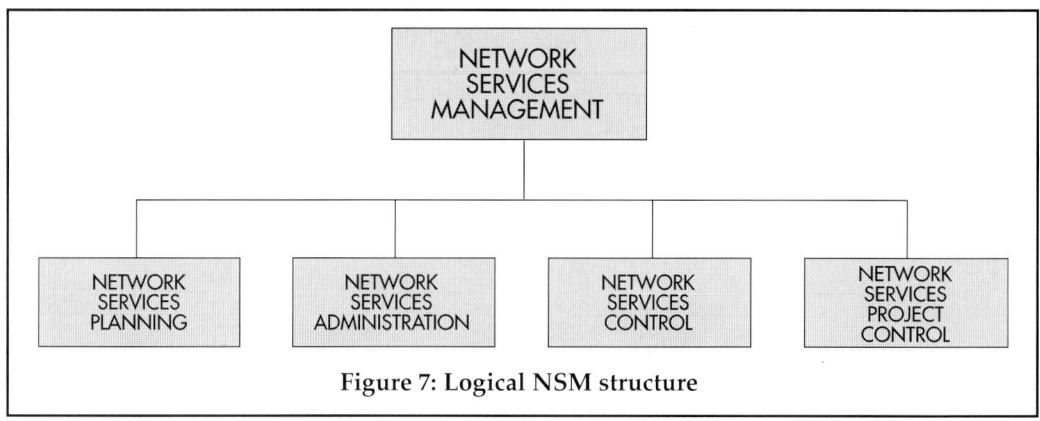

Figure 7: Logical NSM structure

3.0.6 Organizational structure

In larger sites the functions may be the responsibility of separate people, or even separate teams in very large organizations. In small sites all of the functions may be carried out by one person.

Larger organizations

In larger organizations, it may be necessary for the distinct rôle of Network Services Manager, responsible for a number of subsidiary Network Services Management (NSM) functions, to be created. In this case, individual managers or team leaders for each of the subsidiary NSM functions may also be appointed.

Smaller organizations

In smaller organizations, or where there is insufficient requirement for a distinct Network Services Manager, this rôle could be performed by the IT Services Manager or in a distributed organization it may be that the Network Services Manager is also responsible for some of the other Service Management functions such as Change Management and Availability Management.

General

In either case, the rôles would normally reside within the IT Services area. The obvious potential exception is the manager of a voice communications network, a rôle traditionally situated outside the IT Services area. However the implementation of the NSM discipline is the ideal opportunity to integrate the functionality of data and voice network managements into one function, NSM, which is the recommended situation.

3.0.7 Managing an outsourced network

Managing an outsourced network consists of planning and controlling services run on a network that is owned and maintained by another organization. Useful information about this process may be obtained from the **Managing Facilities Management** module. Managed network services masquerade under a number of different names but generally fall into the following classifications:

* Managed Data Network Services (MDNS) - normally used to refer to a network providing data networking facilities to a number of user organizations

* Value Added Network Services (VANS) - generally used to refer to a managed data network service, with additional processing facilities incorporated within the network (eg EDI services)

* Virtual Private Networks (VPNs) - normally refers to voice and PABX network services in which each customer appears to have their own dedicated voice network, whereas in reality they share the network with many other users and connections.

These managed network services can offer a variety of facilities and connections:

* the connection of a number of points that constitute the required network at defined bandwidth levels, eg 64Kbit/s

* the type of transport mechanism required, ie transparent point to point or packet switched (eg X25)

* all moves and changes of connection points carried out on request, either verbally, faxed or via some form of terminal/PC based service management connection

* all problem management and support of the network as part of the service

* in some cases, a limited form of variable bandwidth service is possible between points on the network

* protocol conversion

* some network providers also offer processing facilities and services themselves or gateways to services of other service providers

* interfaces to management information, for example via the SNMP protocol

* total network management may also be offered as part of the service.

The obvious advantage of outsourcing networks is that the day-to-day support and maintenance of the network is carried out externally. This alleviates the need to have skilled staff in-house for this purpose. In addition, the need for investment in a network infrastructure is avoided with consequent savings in capacity and contingency planning.

From a management perspective it allows the business organization to focus on the quality of service provided and the cost of the service to the users. This enables a less ambiguous assessment of the business value of the services provided and used.

Outsourced network services are particularly attractive if the organization requires international network connections.

There may however be much reduced vigilance to improve or rationalize network services or the management of them. Equally seriously, seduction into a non-competitive and costly dependency is likely.

3.0.8 Different rôles of NSM

There are many situations that may arise with regard to the use of managed network services and they will have differing requirements of the NSM function. The main division is between networking and processing (eg mainframe, minicomputer, PC) facilities. These situations are described in the following paragraphs.

All services are in-house — This is probably the most common situation and is the situation considered in the rest of this module, as a complete NSM function is required to run an in-house network.

Part of the network is outsourced but processing is in-house — In this situation part of the network is run in-house and part of the network is outsourced. Again it is likely that a complete NSM function will be required, but the effort required will depend upon how much of the network is outsourced and how much is run in-house. If a significant amount of the network is outsourced then it will be possible to run with a very much reduced level of personnel and functionality.

Section 3
Planning for Network Services Management

All of the network is outsourced but processing is in-house	A very much reduced NSM function will be required in this scenario, as there will be no requirement for any of the NSA, NSC or NSPC functions as these should be provided by the network operator or Facilities Management (FM) organization. There may be a need for an NSP function depending on how much control the organization wishes to retain over planning for future services. The type and quality of service provided by the FM organization or network operator will dictate the amount of work required from an in-house Network Services Manager. However this situation rarely occurs as most organizations run their voice networks in-house, although services specifically targeted at voice networks are now being developed and offered by the network operators.
The network is in-house but the processing is outsourced	As far as NSM is concerned this is the same situation as running all services in-house, except that interfaces will have to be defined and agreed with an external organization.
The network and processing are outsourced	This is the same situation as for all of the network being outsourced except that all negotiations will be with an external organization.
General	Wherever any services are run by FM organizations, the only way to effectively manage the interface between the two organizations is by way of a set of formal Service Level Agreements that govern all aspects of the level and quality of services required. This means that although there is a reduced requirement for the rôle of Network Services Manager, there will be a need to work much more closely with all of the other IT infrastructure management disciplines, especially Service Level Management. So in essence the potential savings in running costs made when outsourcing a network are in the network equipment, links and maintenance costs and in the four supporting disciplines that underpin the Network Services Manager.

3.0.9 The NSM 7-layer model

Traditionally a bottom up approach has been adopted with regard to NSM and network management (ie the network itself is the focus rather than the services it provides), when in reality what is required is a top down approach. The total requirement of the NSM discipline can be represented as seven separate layers of functionality as shown in figure 8.

This model in essence works in a very similar fashion to the ISO 7-Layer model, in that each layer relies upon a service provided by the layer underneath and is a service provider to the layer above. It is essential when establishing an NSM

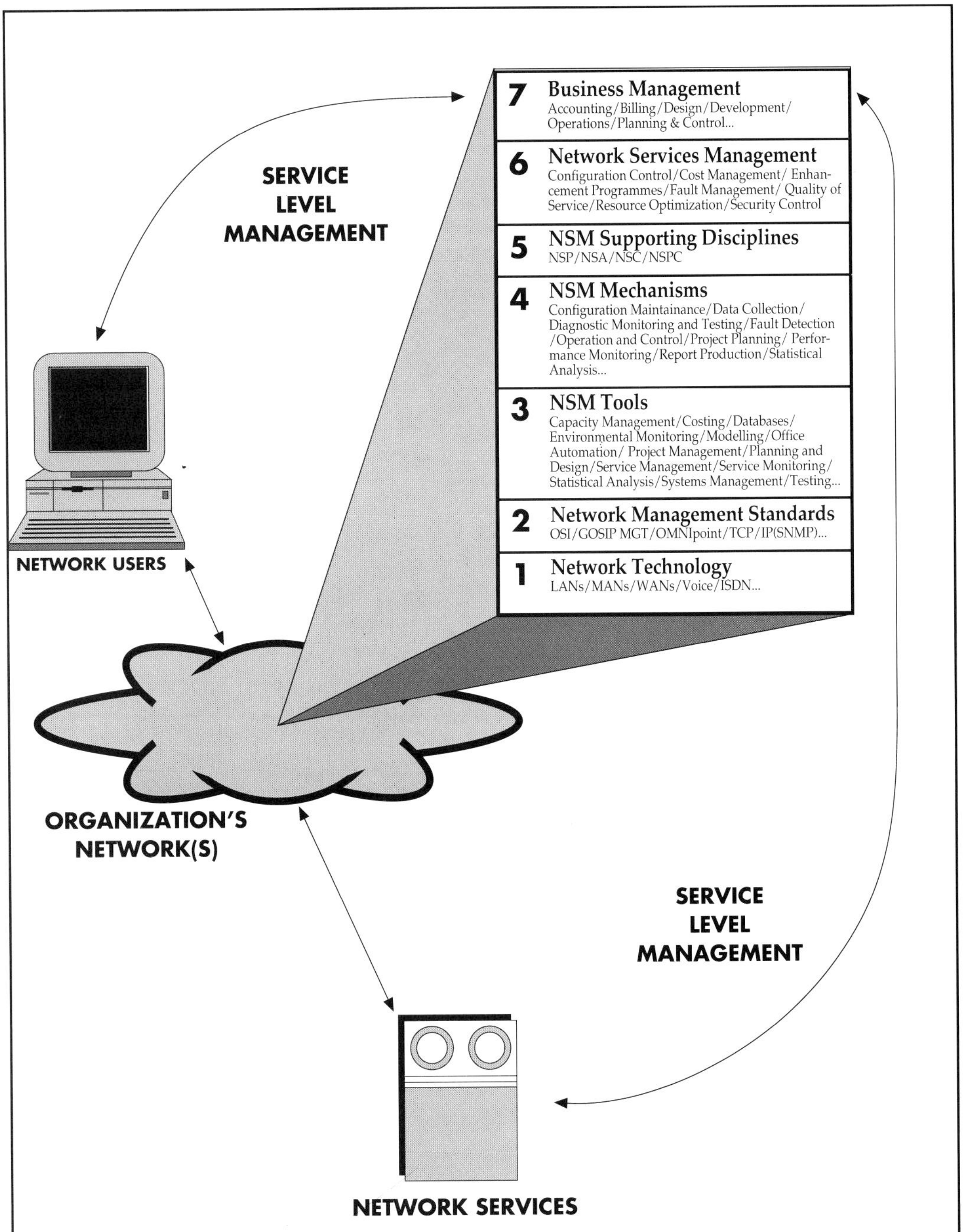

The IT Infrastructure Library
Network Services Management

SERVICE LEVEL MANAGEMENT

NETWORK USERS

ORGANIZATION'S NETWORK(S)

SERVICE LEVEL MANAGEMENT

NETWORK SERVICES

7	**Business Management** Accounting/Billing/Design/Development/Operations/Planning & Control...
6	**Network Services Management** Configuration Control/Cost Management/ Enhancement Programmes/Fault Management/ Quality of Service/Resource Optimization/Security Control
5	**NSM Supporting Disciplines** NSP/NSA/NSC/NSPC
4	**NSM Mechanisms** Configuration Maintainance/Data Collection/Diagnostic Monitoring and Testing/Fault Detection/Operation and Control/Project Planning/ Performance Monitoring/Report Production/Statistical Analysis...
3	**NSM Tools** Capacity Management/Costing/Databases/Environmental Monitoring/Modelling/Office Automation/ Project Management/Planning and Design/Service Management/Service Monitoring/Statistical Analysis/Systems Management/Testing...
2	**Network Management Standards** OSI/GOSIP MGT/OMNIpoint/TCP/IP(SNMP)...
1	**Network Technology** LANs/MANs/WANs/Voice/ISDN...

Figure 8: The NSM 7-layer model

function that a totally integrated approach is adopted, planning NSM from the top layer downwards, ensuring that the emphasis is placed on satisfying the business needs of the organization. This integration process should also apply to the NSM function as a whole so that it is planned as an integral part of the network, and not added on as an afterthought. This will ensure that the NSM staff, tools and procedures will all work in harmony with the network and its technology rather than fighting against it.

The model should be used to ensure than NSM is implemented in an integrated manner, with well defined interfaces and services at the layer boundaries. It is also a good check-list to ensure that all aspects of NSM are addressed.

The functionality of each of the layers is:

Layer 7 - Business Management

This is the top layer of the model and represents the functions needed by the business managers, for example Accounting, Billing, Design, Development, Operations and Planning & Control. Organizations are increasingly dependent upon the swift and reliable operation of their automated information systems. This is especially true where organizations are reliant on the use of front-office systems, ie for supporting direct dealings with their customers. It is essential therefore that the business managers who plan, design and develop the use of these front-office systems are given the tools and the information to facilitate these functions. As the operation of these systems is more visible to the organization's clients and more critical to the operation of the organization, it is essential that they fully satisfy the organization's business requirements in a cost effective manner. They can only be monitored and justified effectively by business managers, using efficient tools, procedures and support from Network Services Management.

Layer 6 - Network Services Management

This layer represents the rôle of the Network Services Manager. It provides the management of the supporting functions in layer 5. It also satisfies the needs of the business managers by supporting the operation of the facilities and information required to optimize the performance of the business management function. The major tasks of this layer are:

* configuration control
* cost management
* fault management and prevention

The IT Infrastructure Library
Network Services Management

* enhancement programmes
* monitoring and improving quality of service
* resource optimization
* security control.

The Network Services Manager is responsible for all of the above NSM activities and is also responsible for:

* the control and integration of all of the network services and users
* the provision of a central point of contact for all aspects of the NSM activities
* the provision of a crucial interface to all business, IT and service managers on all network matters
* ensuring that all network modifications and enhancements have a minimal impact on the continuity of service
* the planning, monitoring and control of the four NSM support disciplines and their environment.

Layer 5 - NSM Supporting Disciplines

These supporting disciplines (as discussed in section 3.0.5) supply the reports and information that the Network Services Manager requires to function in a cost effective manner and to provide the required level of service. These disciplines provide a combined yet structured network support organization for the smooth operation of integrated networks and network services.

Layer 4 - NSM Mechanisms

The mechanisms and procedures that the NSM supporting disciplines are dependent upon constitute layer 4. The main areas where procedures are required are:

* operation and control
* configuration maintenance
* data collection
* diagnostic monitoring and testing
* fault detection and diagnosis
* interfaces to other Service Management functions
* project planning methodology
* performance monitoring
* report production
* statistical analysis.

Section 3
Planning for Network Services Management

Wherever possible manual intervention should be minimized and procedures should be automated and regularly reviewed. These procedures should also be well documented and subject to full Change Management controls. The procedures should also be fully integrated, rather than having stand alone functions. It should be possible for instance, to run performance monitoring procedures that automatically trap certain events, which trigger the running of statistical analysis packages, subsequently causing alarms and reports to be generated. This integration should be accomplished throughout all of the NSM disciplines, so that the procedures help the integration of tools and mechanisms, from both within and outside the NSM function.

Layer 3 - NSM Tools

Layer 3 represents the actual tools that are required within the NSM function. These tools provide the building blocks for the procedures and mechanisms of layer 4 to provide total NSM functionality. The major tool requirements are:

* capacity management tools
* costing tools
* database systems
* environmental monitoring systems
* modelling packages
* office automation systems
* project management packages
* planning and design tools
* service management tools
* service monitoring tools
* statistical analysis packages
* system management systems
* testing tools.

All of the tools utilized within the NSM function should conform to the overall strategies as dictated by the Network Plan as well as conforming to the network management standards and interfaces supported within layer 2. This will then ensure that the procedures to be developed at layer 4 can be fully automated and integrated.

Layer 2 - Network
Management Standards

Layer 2 represents the network management standards, which should be documented in the technical policies of the organization's IS/IT strategies. These standards should be incorporated into all of the products and tools contained in layer 3 to provide an integrated approach to NSM, so that in the long term all the disciplines both inside and outside of NSM can exchange consistent information automatically in a concise and structured manner. The only network management standards and profiles that should be considered are the open and internationally agreed standards:

* GOSIP MGT
* OMNI*Point*
* OSI (CMIS/CMIP)
* TCP/IP (SNMP)
* ITU/TS (formerly CCITT) standards (mainly for voice communications).

More information on these network management protocols can be found in annex F. It is important that organizational standards are adopted as soon as possible, so it is probable that the Network Plan will stipulate that one set of standards (proprietary and/or de facto) is to be adopted currently and for the short term future (because solutions based on these standards are viable), but the long term strategy is to move to another set of standards once they are more stable and more widely supported.

Layer 1 - Network
Technology

Layer 1 provides the physical network connections that allow all of the layers above to communicate. This layer supplies all of the networking technologies:

* ISDNs
* LANs
* MANs
* WANs
* Voice networks.

Not all of these technologies will be in use within every organization, but each organization will probably use more than one. It is imperative that these are not perceived as separate entities, but are seen as an integrated service supporting the business needs of the organization. The NSM function needs to develop the technology strategies within the Network Plan so that physical networks are developed on convergent rather than divergent paths. This

Section 3
Planning for Network Services Management

will enable an integrated approach to be implemented with regard to the associated network management protocols and NSM tools.

The Network Plan

It is essential that the Network Plan contains details of the strategies to be adopted by the organization, in each of the seven layers of the NSM model. These details should cover what is actually achieved in each of the layers currently, what is to be attempted in the short term and what the long term strategy is for each of the layers and areas of NSM functionality.

3.1 Procedures

This section describes the planning which is required for an effective Network Services Management function. Although the following text is written with the assumption that an NSM function does not exist - in common with other IT Infrastructure Library modules - the guidance in section 3 is readily adaptable to any organization, whatever the stage of maturity of their IT infrastructure management.

3.1.1 Initiate project

A project should be initiated and the project team members should be appointed. The Network Services Manager will play a leading rôle in the planning, implementation and ongoing support of network services and should be a prominent member of the project team.

In the case of a green-field site, it is particularly desirable for one project to control not only the planning and design of the network, but also the planning of the NSM function, in order to ensure that effective coordination takes place.

It is recommended that the management of the project follows the CCTA PRINCE method. Use of PRINCE typically divides the work into two distinct stages:

* the feasibility study
* development and implementation.

Project Board

A Project Board should be created. This will provide overall guidance and advice to the project team and will monitor the progress of the project. Recommended Project Board members are:

* Executive - in some case the IT Director, but if a senior business executive can be persuaded, then business interests can be seen to be represented

* Senior User - either a senior manager of the primary group of users or the Service Level Manager acting on behalf of the user community

* Senior Technical - the IT Services Manager.

The Project Board must appoint a project manager, who will manage all aspects of the work and will be responsible for deliverables and progress reports on the project. Other project team members are jointly appointed by the project manager and Project Board. The most important appointment during this stage is that of the Network Services Manager, who will play a leading rôle in the planning and implementation of the NSM function. The Network Services Manager is a likely candidate for the position of project manager. The most likely alternatives are the Manager of Voice Communications, or another senior manager within the IT Services or user areas, such as the Capacity Manager. See annex B for a job description of the Network Services Manager.

3.1.2 Agree objectives & terms of reference of NSM

The objectives and terms of reference of NSM should be discussed and agreed with:

* senior IT management

* senior business management and /or Service Level Manager

* IT Services Managers

* Manager of Voice Communications.

3.1.3 Objectives

Typical objectives include:

* to plan, monitor and control the network element(s) of IT services in order to satisfy business requirements

* to improve the quality of the overall IT service by ensuring that the network element(s) of the IT service achieve(s) the required levels of serviceability, within specified cost constraints

* to propose, introduce and monitor installation standards and procedures that will ensure that required service levels are maintained and where possible improved

Section 3
Planning for Network Services Management

* to monitor and control the service levels provided by relevant network equipment suppliers
* to implement new and modified network services with minimal impact on existing service
* to provide IT and business management with regular reports and reviews on network services targets.

3.1.4 Terms of reference

The terms of reference of NSM are determined by the:

* size, complexity and number of networks in the organization
* nature of the organization's IT systems, ie whether services are provided by centralized or de-centralized systems
* scope of other planned or existing IT infrastructure management functions such as Service Level Management, Capacity Management, Availability Management, Cost Management, Help Desk and Problem Management, Contingency Planning, Configuration and Change Management (further details are contained later within this section).

3.1.4.1 Interfaces

The interfaces between the NSM function and the other IT Service Management disciplines are crucial to the successful operation of the business. The interfaces to be established are indicated in Figure 9 overleaf.

Ideally each of the IT Service Management functions (eg Availability Management) should be completely contained within its own area of responsibility, including all aspects of networking (eg network availability). However because of the diversity and complexity of network issues, this is not always possible and staff are dependent upon the skills of personnel located outside their own discipline. The boundaries between these various functions will vary from organization to organization, and will need to be agreed upon, on a site by site basis. There are two extreme ends of the spectrum.

The **Centralized Multi-Mainframe Site** - the quality of the services of centralized systems will largely be governed by the quality of the services provided by the central processing facility, and network element of the services (but not the administration and control of the network) would typically be managed as part of the main IT Service Management functions.

The IT Infrastructure Library
Network Services Management

The **De-centralized PC Network Site** - in the case of de-centralized systems, particularly those without any centralized elements, the quality of services will be governed by the quality of the network, the overall service quality is not directly related to the services provided by any single processing node, and so IT Service Management rôles may be assigned to the NSM function.

In both cases, there is a need for coordination between centralized (where they exist) and network IT Service Management functions at both the planning and operational levels. However, irrespective of the situation, the NSM areas that need to be considered for each of the IT Service Management functions are discussed in more detail in the following sections. See the appropriate IT Infrastructure Library module for further details of a specific function.

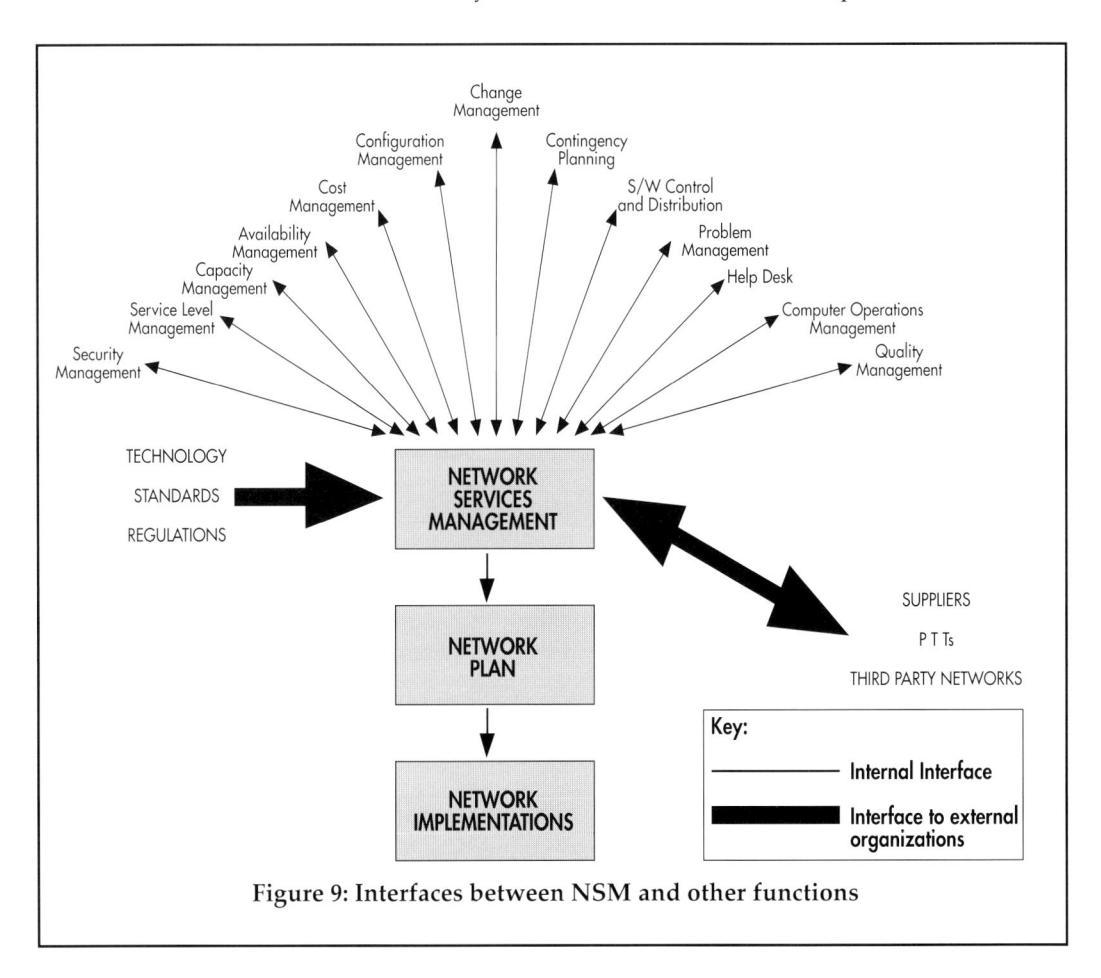

Figure 9: Interfaces between NSM and other functions

3.1.4.2 Availability Management

All of the data which are stored on, processed by, or transmitted over, the network, and services, whether provided by the network or by associated systems (as defined by the scope of the NSM function), should be available, to authorized users at the right level of access, at agreed times as specified by SLAs. Among the options that need to be considered for ensuring the availability of network data and services are:

* for network links and services
    - multiple routes
    - alternate routes
    - use of public networks
    - use of alternate network suppliers (BT, Mercury, etc)
    - triangulated systems

* for network components
    - dial back-up units/modems for leased lines
    - use of digital services such as ISDN for on-demand bandwidth or back-up
    - duplicate systems
    - 'hot standby' systems
    - redundant units and power supplies
    - fall back configurations
    - fault tolerant systems
    - use of mirroring techniques and systems
    - use of duplexing techniques
    - use of error correcting code memory systems
    - use of redundant array of inexpensive discs (RAID) systems and architecture
    - use of uninterruptable power supplies (UPS) and generators
    - use of 'hot card' swap systems
    - use of on-site spares holding

The IT Infrastructure Library
Network Services Management

- identification of potential hire sources
- committed supply arrangements with preferred suppliers.

3.1.4.3 Capacity Management

The information relating to network performance should always be located in the Network Database (NDB), within the main Capacity Management Database (CDB). The control of the NDB and CDB clearly being under the direction of the Capacity Management function, although responsibility for the collection and analysis of the information will generally reside within the NSM function. Details of network performance monitoring and analysis and the network tools that are available, are contained within the **Capacity Management** module and in annex E of this module.

3.1.4.4 Change Management

The NSM function must operate under a Change Management system for all network hardware, software and documentation, and the NSM function should be represented at the Change Advisory Board (CAB) meetings.

In a de-centralized system, the network and network management system would assist in automating the change management system. As Change Management is inextricably combined with Configuration Management, it is desirable that the same automated system is used for both functions. However, well-defined procedures can at least partially overcome any shortcomings (eg lack of integration) of tools.

3.1.4.5 Configuration Management

It is essential that Configuration Management (CM) is controlled centrally. However, there are significant advantages to be gained through the use of network management tools to automatically maintain network (and connected systems) configuration information. Therefore the NSM function will usually have the responsibility for supplying the network Configuration Management information, and so effective co-ordination between NSM and CM is vital. However the Configuration Management function must retain control of all of the information located within the Configuration Management Database (CMDB). Ideally this process of information transfer between the network management systems and the CMDB should be fully automated.

Section 3
Planning for Network Services Management

Where a system is de-centralized, the network and network management system should be used to provide a CMDB. As Configuration Management is inextricably combined with Change Management it is desirable that the same automated system is used for both functions. However, well-defined procedures can at least partially overcome any shortcomings (eg lack of integration) of tools.

3.1.4.6 Contingency Planning

For centralized local networks within, say, a single building, the responsibility for disaster recovery planning (ie total physical loss) should reside with a separate Contingency Planning (CP) function. Planning for other serious, but not total, losses in service is usually catered for by careful network design and is therefore the responsibility of NSM.

For large de-centralized networks, or where telecommunications is the sole or major service provided, NSM needs to be intimately involved in CP, and may ultimately be responsible for providing CP. It is essential for the Contingency Plan to cover all of the critical elements of total service provision. This means that it is not sufficient to have a plan that documents the recovery from disasters to critical host services only. A complete Business Contingency Plan (or Business Continuity Plan) will be needed, covering all of the critical elements necessary to providing continuity of service to the business. This will necessitate the completion of a much more detailed business impact analysis and risk analysis covering the priority and criticality of each terminal and each user (or group of terminals and group of users) of the system. CCTA advises the use of the CCTA Risk Analysis and Management Method (CRAMM) to conduct risk analysis.

This would also involve a more detailed analysis of all of the possible critical areas of failure within networked services:

* host services and host service equipment
* distributed services and distributed service equipment
* major network nodes and networking equipment (eg switches)
* major network gateways
* PABXs
* major sites and buildings
* network connections to hot standby sites
* terminal systems and PC networks.

Large, distributed networks may necessitate the consideration of a multi-layer approach to disaster recovery, using regionalized or localized disaster recovery plans and teams, on either a site by site, or region by region basis. Local teams to handle on site disasters at remote sites may be required to run under the control and direction of a centrally based Emergency Control Centre (ECC). Staffing of the ECC may be on a permanent basis, if the workload dictates, but is more likely to be staffed on-demand when disasters occur. In the latter case, priorities and back-up arrangements for staff must be clearly defined in advance. The multi-layer approach would enable the central team to act as back-up and support of the local team (eg for impact assessment), whilst the local team are on hand for the local issues on the affected site (such as detection, damage assessment and escalation). However if such a system is to function effectively then the responsibilities must be clearly defined and hard copies of the appropriate disaster recovery plans must be stored as follows:

* at the central site (Emergency Control Centre)
* in off-site secure fire safes
* at each remote site or regional centre, preferably with duplicates stored in a local off-site secure fire safe
* at each hot standby site.

All of these copies are additional to the usual circulation lists for centralized systems and this makes the processes of copy control, distribution and change control even more complicated, but even more essential.

3.1.4.7 Cost Management

The major problem to be overcome is equitable charging for a backbone network, especially where it is providing ISDN functionality. However the following options are available.

Direct charging — This method would involve charging on a site by site, or department by department basis for the network equipment and links installed.

Network usage — Charges to users would be based on, and directly related to, their respective network usage, either:

* packets transferred for data
* numbers and duration of calls for voice.

Apportionment	The total network charges would be divided between the various user sections and departments, either:

        * equally

        * based on duration of calls

        * based on their usage of networked services, such as host processing

but only indirectly related to usage of the network itself.

Per connection	This is just a different method of apportionment based on a set charge per connection for:

        * each PC/terminal/printer for data/ISDN

        * each handset/fax etc. for voice.

The most common form of overall network charging policy is a combination of two or more of the above methods, for example a fixed annual connection charge and monitored usage charges (cf BT's UK charges).

3.1.4.8 Help Desk and Problem Management

The concept of a single (logical) Help Desk is strongly advised within the IT Infrastructure Library. The provision of a separate Help Desk facility for network services is not advised because of the increased complexity it presents to the users of the service, the duplication of effort that is required to provide the Help Desk, and the increased difficulty in handling incidents and problems effectively. It is also confusing to users, deciding which Help Desk to contact, as it is not always immediately obvious. The Help Desk, Computer Operations and Network Services Control staff are commonly combined into a single Operations Bridge area, thereby locating as many elements as possible together, in an attempt to improve the incident response times to users.

The normal interface between the Help Desk and NSM will be provided by NSC on a day-to-day basis. However for serious incidents and major problems, Problem Management will escalate the situation to involve other areas of NSM.

Where a (physically) distributed Help Desk is in use then NSM will be responsible for providing the network service that supports the operation of the distributed Help Desk and there will obviously need to be close liaison between the NSM, Help Desk and Problem Management functions.

3.1.4.9 Security

There are two major issues of network security, other than Availability, which is covered in 3.1.4.2, which need to be investigated.

Confidentiality - ensuring that all of the data which are stored on, processed by, or transmitted over, the network, and services, whether provided by the network or by associated systems (as defined by the scope of the NSM function), are only available to authorized users at the right level of access.

Integrity - ensuring that all data and services associated with the network, and the network itself, are free from corruption and malicious software.

Ideally the NSM function should assume responsibility for these issues and report back to the organization's IT Security Officer on progress.

For further guidance on network security issues, see the **IT Security Library** volume on **Network Security**.

3.1.4.10 Service Level Management

Service Level Management (SLM) should always be separate from NSM. NSM needs to be aware of, and contribute to, all Service Level Agreements (SLAs) that contain a network element, should monitor them and supply regular exception reports to SLM on all breaches of network SLAs. The NSM function should also receive copies of all reports and minutes from service review meetings. The NSM function should also be aware of the Service Improvement Programme (SIP) and its contents and be active in its implementation.

3.1.4.11 Software Control and Distribution

The relationship between the Software Control and Distribution (SC&D) and NSM functions is a complicated one, in that NSM should not only be the provider of some of the SC&D services, it should also be a user - to control the distribution of network software. It is therefore essential that a close relationship exists between SC&D and NSM. SC&D must be operated centrally with overall responsibility for maintaining the Definitive Software Library (DSL) and for determining software release policies within the organization. The NSM function must conform to all of the organization's SC&D procedures.

Section 3
Planning for Network Services Management

NSM should be responsible for providing the mechanisms for enabling the distribution of software to all sites within the organization. NSM should also maintain an independent network test environment for the testing of network hardware upgrades and new network software releases - see the **Testing an IT Service for Operational Use** module for more details.

3.1.5 Initiate feasibility study

A feasibility study should be undertaken to establish the importance of NSM to the business. The feasibility study should concentrate on examining the following issues:

* the extent to which NSM is currently practised
* if the introduction or improvement of NSM is likely to be cost effective and bring benefits
* whether suitable staff and other resources (eg funding, tools) are available
* if senior management are committed to the introduction or improvement of NSM
* when to implement NSM in relation to the other Service Management functions.

The effective management of network services can be a vital function of an organization. A feasibility study for its introduction or improvement should therefore focus on the positive effects of introducing the function and examine what the organization will achieve through operating such a function. This should be contrasted with the impact on the business of not running an NSM function.

The feasibility study is best split into four parts:

* produce a framework description (3.1.5.1) for the introduction or improvement of NSM including costs
* review the current function (3.1.5.2)
* perform a gap analysis (3.1.5.3)
* produce a feasibility report (3.1.5.4), recommending (or not) the creation or improvement of NSM.

3.1.5.1 Framework description

A framework description should be produced for the introduction or improvement of NSM. The framework description should be based on the aims and objectives and, in effect, constitutes a business case describing the desired state of NSM in some detail. The benefits to the business, together with requirements, an outline project plan and costs should be highlighted for senior management. The framework description will almost certainly be incorporated in the feasibility study report.

The framework description should, as a minimum, describe:

* current, and desirable changes to, organizational policies

* the scope of NSM and interfaces to other IT Service Management areas

* procedures for the operation of NSM

* numbers, rôles and responsibilities of staff involved with NSM

* the current status and expected development of SLAs, service objectives and performance criteria, ie does the organization adhere to, or intend to adhere to SLAs

* IT management information required from, and supplied to, Capacity Management, to assess the effectiveness and efficiency of the Capacity Management function in processing network information

* the information required by and presented to the Cost Management and Service Level Management functions

* the scope of the network, ie does 'network' include file and mail servers, print servers, printers and other I/O devices, system software, PC gateways, voice systems, communications processors etc, ideally it should cover all of these systems

* details of tools required

* the contents of the network database (NDB), covering both technical and business related data

* expectations of regular and exception reporting facilities required from monitoring tools and the NDB at the operational, tactical and strategic levels

* accommodation and environment requirements

* an outline project plan, stating activities, end-products, controls, organization and required resources

* budgetary estimates of expenditure based on the outline project plan.

3.1.5.2 Review current function

Where network management is currently practised in the organization a review should be conducted to 'establish details of the staff, processes, procedures and tools in use. These details are needed for analysis of the gap between the required functionality and the current functionality. The review should be sufficiently detailed to allow a detailed project plan to be produced.

The review should address the following topics:

* the procedures currently in place and their effectiveness
* who is responsible for existing NSM activities (if any) - this may be informal rather than part of job descriptions
* the tools currently in use and their effectiveness
* current customer satisfaction with the present situation; this should focus on those users most affected, ie those users with the most stringent network performance and availability requirements and those users with the largest demand for network capacity
* current and desired requirements by other IT Service Management areas, such as Service Level Management, Capacity, Availability, Cost Management and Contingency Planning
* current budget, cost effectiveness and assessment of value for money by the customer if currently paying (directly or indirectly) for network services.

3.1.5.3 Gap analysis

The gap analysis should:

* identify the major differences between the current functionality and the required functionality of NSM
* if the gap between the current and the required functionality is large, identify separate phases, specifying the required functionality, staff, procedures and support tools at each phase. Each phase can then be treated as a separate implementation stage or project.

For each phase a separate description of the objectives, required functionality and order of implementation should be produced. The following should be covered:

* establish/improve NSM function
    - production of a catalogue of network services
    - development of network charging mechanisms
    - setting of initial service levels or service level targets (where none exist at present; these are not to be included in SLAs initially)
* establish/improve NSP function
    - production of a Network Plan
    - development of network contingency plans
    - completion of network business impact analysis and risk analysis exercises, and incorporation of networking aspects into availability improvement
    - construction of network database (NDB) and data capture mechanisms, and the integration of networking into the capacity plan
* establish/improve NSA function
    - implementation of SC&D release, distribution and implementation procedures for network software
    - implementation of all Configuration and Change Management procedures
* establish/improve NSC function
    - basic incident control and rectification, integrated into the Help Desk, Problem, Change and Configuration Management processes.

3.1.5.4 Produce feasibility report

A management report, including data from the framework description, current systems review and gap analysis, should be produced at the conclusion of the feasibility study. The feasibility study report should be submitted to the IT Services Manager and to the Project Board for approval. The report should include:

* an assessment of the current situation with regard to the services which are being provided, and to the future situation with NSM

Section 3
Planning for Network Services Management

* a statement of all problems which need to be addressed, eg lack of communication, lack of relevant information or capacity

* the need for the introduction or improvement of NSM within the organization and the justification outlining the benefits which can be expected - section 6 gives guidance on this subject (note that it does not necessarily follow that the separate NSM disciplines need to be laboriously considered by all organizations, particularly those with small LANs and no predicted growth)

* recommendations on how to implement NSM within the organization (this section should include any prerequisites or constraints in terms of organizational structure or culture)

* examples of prototype reports which could be produced by NSM to stimulate reaction from the target recipients

* a brief project plan, showing timescales, staffing levels, costs and also specifying the objectives, main tasks, dependencies, interfaces, ongoing operations, and deliverables of each phase of the project

* recommendations on tools to support NSM

* a management summary which compares and contrasts the costs of not managing network services effectively, with the costs of implementing NSM.

3.1.6 Obtain approval

The approval of the Project Board, together with the commitment from senior management for the necessary resources (which might be substantial), must be obtained before further progress is made.

3.1.7 Produce project plan

A detailed project plan should now be produced defining the order in which the phases identified by the gap analysis are to be implemented. Each phase should have a detailed plan, with implementation timescales and regular reviews, as well as details of the metrics to be used and the targets to be achieved, which should be related to the objectives (see section 3.1.3).

The plan should also contain details of changes to the organizational structure, together with job descriptions and responsibilities of each proposed post. Suggested job descriptions are contained in annex B. Details of training schedules for each member of staff involved within the plan should also be documented. Further information on planning organizational structures is contained in the **IT Services Organization** module.

3.1.8 Plan operational responsibilities and procedures

Management of the network systems and services is achieved by having well defined and documented responsibilities and procedures. These cover all aspects of running, supporting and managing network services and include:

* procedures for planning, monitoring, controlling and implementing networks

* procedures for communicating and interfacing with other Service Management functions.

The operational procedures required for the network services management function fall into four main areas of responsibility:

* Network Services Planning (NSP)

* Network Services Administration (NSA)

* Network Services Control (NSC)

* Network Services Project Control (NSPC).

The following sub-sections define the procedures and responsibilities for each of these areas.

3.1.8.1 Network Services Planning

Objective

The objective of the Network Services Planning (NSP) function is:

"Planning the provision of new or modified network services to meet business requirements, as defined by the Business and IS Strategies, with minimal disruption to existing services and users".

Responsibilities

The major responsibilities of NSP are to produce the Network Plan and agree the future requirements for networking services with all other planning functions within the organization, especially Infrastructure Planning. NSP should then review alternative proposals and select the most appropriate solution that conforms with the organization's Network Plan. NSP is also responsible for planning the scope of the other NSM functions and their interfaces with other parts of the IT Directorate. NSP must

Section 3
Planning for Network Services Management

	regularly review and revise the Network Plan in synchronization with the Business, IS and IT Plans - see the **Planning and Control** module for further details.
Major tasks	See annex B for a list of the major tasks of NSP.
The Network Plan	The Network Plan should be reviewed and revised annually, or following the release of new Business, IS or IT Plans. Preferably the plans should all be reviewed within the same timeframe, in conjunction with other Service Management plans (particularly the Capacity Plan) as they are inter-dependent. The Network Plan, which is complementary to all of the other plans, should cover the changing requirements for networks and network services, evolving from the requirements of the business and IT. It should, wherever possible, contain alternative options.
Information collection	Discussions must be held with a number of people and procedures must be established for the collection of information for the Network Plan:

* the business managers for information on the Business Strategy and Plan, and the customer demands for growth in networking requirements

* the Service Level Management function for user, business and SLA requirements for current and future needs

* Availability Management for network availability requirements, both current and future

* Capacity Management for details of the current and future requirements of network capacity, traffic, performance and responses

* Cost Management for the implications of the various network options

* Contingency Planning for details on the current and future networking requirements for disaster recovery

* Configuration and Change Management for any additional network requirements

* Help Desk and Problem Management for any additional network requirements

* Software Control & Distribution to determine whether there are likely to be any new network mechanisms needed or any changes to the release policies

The IT Infrastructure Library
Network Services Management

* IT Security Officer for the organization's IT Security Policy, Network Security Policy and any new security procedures or requirements

* applications development teams for new or enhanced services requirements

* those managing relationships with external suppliers for any changes to conditions.

Timescale
The Network Plan should cover a period of two to three years, with more detailed information on the first six to twelve months. It should be reviewed and revised annually or possibly every six months for a very volatile organization, but is best reviewed in conjunction with the Business and IS Plans of the organization.

Contents of the plan
The Network Plan should contain the following:

* a management summary with recommendations and preferred strategies, suppliers and solutions

* details of the current networks

    - network schematics
    - servers, users and methods of access
    - locations and types of connections
    - network performance and traffic
    - standards, protocols and interfaces
    - network management systems and tools
    - network and user availability levels and requirements
    - disaster recovery connections to hot start sites
    - security mechanisms
    - support and maintenance arrangements

* details of the future network requirements, under the same headings as current networks, and their planned timeframe

* network and telecommunications strategies of the organization, with regard to technology, standards and interfaces as follows

    - backbone networks
    - voice networks
    - local area networks (LANs)

Section 3
Planning for Network Services Management

- wide area networks (WANs)
- metropolitan area networks (MANs)
- integrated digital services such as ISDN
- network gateways
- cabling
- video
- imaging
- third party networks (PTTs and VANs)
- PCs and terminals
- network servers and services (eg Print servers, file servers, E-mail and fax)
- network management systems

* details of the long term networking strategy with particular reference to the NSM 7-layer model
* details of alternative short term network scenarios with budgetary costs, business impact, advantages and disadvantages
* detailed network recommendations.

The Network Plan should cover all of the topics above, unless the subjects are covered elsewhere or are not relevant, in which case this should be explicitly stated within the plan.

3.1.8.2 Network Services Administration

Objective

The objective of the Network Services Administration (NSA) function is:

"To provide technical support and information analysis and reports, on the operational and managerial activities within the NSM function, and on the performance of the NSM function as a whole".

Responsibilities

The principal responsibilities of NSA are to provide a pool of in-depth technical expertise and to provide analysis and reporting, to management, on all aspects of the organization's network.

The IT Infrastructure Library
Network Services Management

Technical expertise	NSA staff will have an in-depth technical knowledge of network:

* equipment
* software
* protocols
* connections

in use within the organization.

Management reporting	The majority of the managerial information prepared regularly by NSA is for two intended audiences, IT Services Management and Business Managers. Management summaries should also be produced for the IS Steering Committee, at least twice a year, highlighting the costs and benefits of the NSM function.

IT Services Management requires information on the underlying performance of the network, usually on a monthly basis. This information includes the actual performance and usage of the network services and associated support services rather than just the perceived availability and performance. The reports must include information on the resources used on a 'per account group basis', for charge back purposes and details of all breaches of SLA targets. Details of trends in usage, performance and incidents on all network equipment should also be produced.

The format and consistency of the reports can be greatly enhanced by automating much of the data collection, analysis and report preparation using network management systems, statistical analysis packages and spreadsheet packages. These reports will also provide most of the information and analysis on the effectiveness of all aspects of the NSM function.

Exception reports	As well as providing reports on a regular basis NSA will be responsible for providing exception reports on an ad-hoc basis. The types of exception reports required are likely to be:

Breaches of SLA target reports (ie reacting to breaches in SLAs) - all breaches of any aspect of an SLA should be reported as soon as they have been identified, containing details of the SLA, the shortfall, dates, times and locations of the incident(s). These should be circulated to NSM, SLM and interested IT Management.

Capacity threshold exceptions (ie proactive warning of potential breaches in SLAs) - threshold response times, utilizations and error levels should be set for all network resources. Whenever they are exceeded then exception reports should be generated containing details of the date and time of the exception, and details of the resource, the location, the threshold and the amount by which it has been exceeded. These reports should be circulated to NSM, Capacity Management, NSP, and other interested IT Management.

Network incident response and repair times

Response times and repair times should be recorded in the CMDB for all network equipment. Exception reports should be generated every time that either the target or minimum response or repair time has not been met for a particular incident, or the volume of incidents exceeds the threshold for a given unit. These reports should be circulated to NSM, Availability Management and other interested IT Management.

Interfaces to other areas

NSA will provide the technical interface to all other aspects of IT and IT Service Management. NSA will additionally be responsible for urgent and intermediate changes, required for Configuration and Capacity modifications, ensuring that Change Management and SC&D procedures are adhered to at all times. The maintenance of all NSM documentation and procedures also falls within the remit of NSA and again all documentation should be under the control of Configuration and Change Management procedures.

Major tasks

See annex B for a list of the major tasks of NSA.

3.1.8.3 Network Services Control

Objective

The objective of the Network Services Control (NSC) function is:

"To provide day-to-day support on the operation and control of all network equipment in use within the organization."

Responsibilities

NSC staff will have an in-depth knowledge of all aspects of operation and control of the networking equipment in use within the organization. Their responsibilities include making minor changes to the network infrastructure requested via the Change Management procedures and investigation of incident reports. NSC will provide second line technical support to the Help Desk on service incidents and problems. NSC will also provide incident control for network incidents, including informing the Help Desk and recording incidents on the incident control system.

Minor changes to live systems and performance tuning will

The IT Infrastructure Library
Network Services Management

also be carried out by NSC. The scope of these changes will be detailed within strictly defined limits, under delegation from Change Management.

NSC will also provide specialist support to the Problem Management function in the handling of complex or difficult incidents or problems. NSC will act as the day-to-day technical contact point for the engineers and technical support staff of external maintenance and support organizations.

NSC are responsible for ensuring that all operational documentation for systems and services is kept up to date.

NSC provide the foundation data for the creation of the Network Database(s). These are required to enable the current network services to be fully managed and supported, and future network services as demanded by business needs to be planned.

Maintaining the security of a network service is an on-going process. NSC are responsible for monitoring the network in order to detect and investigate any breaches of security that occur either by accident or design. NSC are responsible for reporting all security breaches and all attempted security breaches to the organization's IT Security Officer who is responsible for taking follow-up action to deal with offenders and tighten up procedures (including the use of unlicenced and unauthorized PC software and the detection of computer virus attacks).

Major tasks — See annex B for a list of the major tasks of NSC.

3.1.8.4 Network Services Project Control

Objective — The objective of the Network Services Project Control (NSPC) function is:

"To provide the project management and control of major new network or network enhancement installation programmes".

Responsibilities — NSPC are responsible for the development of project plans for all major network projects, either for the purposes of new network installations or significant network enhancements or upgrades. In the majority of organizations this will not be a permanent function but is likely to be staffed by personnel seconded from other networking disciplines. In larger organizations, or where the network is particularly volatile, there may be a person, if not a team, permanently allocated to the function. These responsibilities may be shared with the IT Planning Unit, where one exists.

Section 3
Planning for Network Services Management

Organization	The NSPC staff and its associated project team need to be organizationally separate from the operational staff to ensure that:

* the current operational workload does not interfere with installation work

* the installation project is properly managed; this requires skills which may not be fully developed in the operational team

* there is a defined end-date by which the project must be signed off

* separate teams exist to allow independent quality reviews to be undertaken.

The processes involved in a project for the planning and implementation of a new network service are detailed in annex G. However as a minimum the project plans must contain details of the following:

* impact assessment of the planned changes

* resource requirements

* priority and timescale

* build plans

* back-out plans

* testing plans

* distribution plans

* implementation plans

* plans for Change Management authorization

* review intervals and schedules

* sign off and handover

* training of IT and user staff.

Training	The installation period is the best time to train NSM and Help Desk staff on new or enhanced networks and services. The ideal way of achieving this is to second staff to the installation project as part of the project resource. This has the double benefit of familiarizing personnel with the equipment and its operation whilst contributing to the overall objectives and progress of the project.

Staff should be given the opportunity to acquaint themselves with new:

* procedures
* network management systems
* network hardware and software
* external services access points
* manuals and documentation
* suppliers and PTTs
* technology.

Major tasks   See annex B for a list of the major tasks of NSPC.

3.1.9 Select support tools

Choose the support tools required by the NSM function using the guidance provided in section 7. The selection of tools is driven by the need to enhance or facilitate NSM. The ability to exchange information with other Service Management tools is essential to the efficient and smooth operation of NSM. Until recently the only method of achieving this was to implement a proprietary set of network and Service Management tools. However developments and emerging standards from the Network Management Forum (NMF) have encouraged the development of network management and Service Management tools that exchange information automatically. The implementation of NSM is an ideal opportunity to review the use of Service Management tools within the organization, and possibly move towards tools and systems that are more integrated.

3.1.10 Plan staff training

Network staff need to be trained in NSM and also given an appreciation of all Service Management functions.

Network related   NSM staff need to be familiarized with:

* their new responsibilities
* the new NSM functions and interfaces
* the new network management systems and support tools
* the new responsibilities and interfaces to the Service Management functions
* any new networks and service access points.

Section 3
Planning for Network Services Management

For greenfield sites, it is useful to exercise the service management procedures on some trial users before the network goes live.

General Service Management

The second training requirement is in Service Management in general. All NSM staff should be given an appreciation of each of the Service Management disciplines. This could be consolidated by secondment to one or more of the Service Management areas during the implementation of the NSM function, to assist that discipline to adjust to the new NSM functions. Whenever possible, the opportunity should be taken for NSM staff to be involved with or assist in:

* test procedures and practices
* Capacity Management
* incident control and Problem Management
* Configuration/Change Management
* Contingency Planning
* Security monitoring and reporting
* Cost Management
* Service Level Management
* Availability Management
* Software Control & Distribution

3.1.11 Select/design accommodation & environment

There are a range of organizational, technical and ergonomic issues involved in the successful creation of NSM.

It is preferable to keep the NSC, Computer Operations (if any), the Help Desk and possibly NSA functions collocated, for instance in an Operations Bridge area, in order to maximize communications. However, it is important to maintain a managerial separation to ensure that rôles and responsibilities do not become blurred.

This is not to suggest that only centralized management is possible or preferable. The ultimate test for NSM procedures and methods is whether they will still work if other Service Management functions (or parts of NSM) are geographically separate. Dependence on the local knowledge of specific staff members should be avoided by documenting procedures and storing relevant information.

For guidance on accommodation design, see the **Office Design and Planning** module.

3.1.12 Plan reviews and audits

Plans must be made for regular reviews and audits of the network and NSM function to check that it is adhering to laid-down procedures. See section 5 for more details.

3.1.13 Review implementation plan

The NSM implementation plan should be circulated to senior IT management for final approval and sign-off.

3.2 Dependencies

Planning the implementation of the NSM function requires support from many groups and functions within IT Services. It is recommended that interfaces are developed with the following functions, which should be planned as part of the NSM implementation project if they do not already exist:

* Configuration and Change Management
* Service Level Management
* Capacity and Availability Management
* Help Desk and Problem Management
* Software Development
* Procurement
* Security.

The successful planning of the NSM function will also depend upon several other factors:

* the commitment of senior management
* staff with adequate network skills and experience
* sufficient funds allocated in the budget for the initial project and the subsequent annual running costs of the NSM function
* having a clear understanding of the technical networking issues (eg regulations and standards to be observed) and their relationship to Business and IS Strategies
* knowledge of the business implications of the technological options.

Section 3
Planning for Network Services Management

3.3 People

3.3.1 Duties and qualifications

Note that in smaller organizations, or organizations with relatively small networks (which could mean local networks with hundreds of PCs), one person may be responsible for many or all of the duties described in this section.

For detailed job descriptions, see annex B.

Network Services Manager

The Network Services Manager is required to ensure that the network service requirements of the organization are met and to advise senior IT Management accordingly. He/she should have:

* networking knowledge - a good all round knowledge of networking principles, practices and technologies, including network management systems

* an understanding of the IT Service Management disciplines, their respective responsibilities, and their effect on the IT organization and procedures - preferably an appreciation of the IT Infrastructure Library

* the Information Systems Examination Board (ISEB) certificate in IT Infrastructure Management and/or Telecommunications Management, or equivalent

* communications skills - the ability to obtain, analyse and pass information to managers inside and outside IT Services

* IT expertise - the ability to comprehend computer hardware, software, networks, distributed systems, PCs and their use and be conversant with their environmental requirements

* business awareness - the ability to understand the organization's business and translate business networking requirements into networking technology requirements

* contractual knowledge - an understanding of legal and contractual requirements of suppliers' contracts

* knowledge of statistics, mathematics and accounting methods

The IT Infrastructure Library
Network Services Management

* managerial skills - experience of resource management, supervisory techniques, budgeting and planning; in large installations the Network Services Manager will be in charge of a team and will therefore require people management skills.

The Network Services Manager will also be responsible for coordinating the four supporting disciplines of NSM:

* Network Services Planning (NSP)
* Network Services Administration (NSA)
* Network Services Control (NSC)
* Network Services Project Control (NSPC).

Network Services Planner The main activity of the Network Services Planning (NSP) function is to plan the provision of new or modified network services which meet business requirements, as defined by the Business Strategy, with minimal disruption to existing services and users. A Network Services Planner needs:

* knowledge of IT Service Management
* knowledge of networking concepts, interfaces and technologies
* planning and costing skills
* network design skills
* communications and general IT training and experience
* an understanding of project management and control procedures, such as PRINCE.

Network Services Administrator Network Services Administration (NSA) are responsible for providing technical support and information analysis and reporting, on the operational and managerial activities within the NSM function, and on the performance of the NSM function as a whole. Network Services Administrators also conduct site surveys of all new network sites and they therefore need the following skills:

* knowledge of networking concepts, interfaces and technologies
* network operations skills
* network diagnostic skills
* knowledge of environmental requirements
* an in-depth technical knowledge of network equipment, protocols, software and connections.

Section 3
Planning for Network Services Management

Network Services Controller
: The Network Services Control (NSC) function provides day-to-day support on the operation and control of all network equipment in use within the organization. Network Services Controllers should have:

* an in-depth knowledge of all aspects of operation and control of the networking equipment in use within the organization

* knowledge of networking concepts, interfaces and technologies

* network operations skills

* network diagnostic skills.

Network Services Project Controller
: The main activity of Network Services Project Control (NSPC) is to provide the project management and control of major new network or network enhancement installation programmes. A Network Services Project Controller should have:

* knowledge of networking concepts, interfaces and technologies

* project management and project control skills, such as PRINCE

* experience of computer project management packages

* good interpersonal communications skills.

The job descriptions of the Network Services Manager and the supporting disciplines are contained in annex B.

3.3.2 Training

The Network Services Manager must ensure that all staff have their training needs assessed and matched against any likely demands placed upon them from the installation of the new function. A planned training schedule should be developed to take account of this assessment. The training may take differing forms:

* network related - the training of members of the NSA and NSC functions, possibly leading to the ISEB certificate in Telecommunications Management, may be completed prior to and during implementation of the NSM function

* customer support - (ie Help Desk and Operations) training and appreciation of new services, may be completed prior to and during the implementation or may form part of an existing cross-training procedure

* infrastructure/Service Management related - training of NSM staff in an appreciation of all Service Management functions, leading to the ISEB certificate in IT Infrastructure Management.

It is necessary to have a basic understanding of network services and systems and to maintain an up-to-date knowledge of network management techniques, equipment, standards and technologies. This understanding may be obtained by:

* regularly attending relevant exhibitions and conferences
* attending network seminars
* attending supplier courses and seminars
* reading networking journals and magazines and other relevant publications
* contracting-in external skills and resources
* 'in-house' presentations
* secondments to other areas of IT such as Capacity Management and Availability Management.

3.3.3 Other personnel

Computer Operations, Service Level Management, the Help Desk, Configuration Management, Cost Management, Capacity Management, Availability Management, Contingency Planning and Security Management staff must be involved as appropriate. Their involvement is an essential component of the planning process and will ensure their early cooperation and reduce the possibility of resistance to change later on.

If the Network Services Manager has either a skills or resource shortage that cannot be internally met, then the use of consultancy may be considered.

One type of consultancy which is of particular relevance to Network Services Managers is network troubleshooting. Some companies operate a service for which no charge is made until the problem is solved, charges being subject to overall ceilings. Use of such a service enables managers to deal with problems which are beyond the expertise of the regular staff but within a fixed budget.

Section 3
Planning for Network Services Management

3.4 Timing

General

Organizations should ensure that sufficient time is allocated to the task of designing and implementing the technology, and planning and implementing the management and support infrastructures. Estimates of the time needed to implement NSM will vary considerably and will depend upon:

* the extent to which IT Service Management is already practised
* the size, complexity and number of networks in the organization
* the nature of the organization's IT systems
* the number of systems to be covered by the NSM function.

Greenfield site

In a greenfield installation it will take some six months to a year (following implementation of the network) to develop an NSM function depending upon:

* the availability of network management systems and NSM tools
* the level of detail required in the collection of network data
* the amount of effort required to monitor the compliance to requirements
* the expertise and experience of the staff involved.

Pilot

As has been stated previously, NSM is best implemented in a series of steps or stages. The best way of implementing the function is to run a pilot exercise of the NSM function coincidental with a new network installation or a move to a new building. This should also be scheduled in conjunction with a relatively slack period of business, if possible.

Other IT Service Management disciplines

The only other aspect of timing to be considered is the implementation of the NSM function in relation to the other IT Service Management disciplines. NSM is considered to be one of the disciplines contributing to short-term operational goals and should therefore be implemented before the disciplines that contribute to medium-term tactical goals eg Cost, Capacity and Availability Management. Automated Configuration Management underpins the operation of all of the disciplines and should therefore be implemented first, probably in conjunction with Change Management. It would therefore seem logical to implement NSM somewhere between these two sets of disciplines, probably in conjunction with the Management of Local Processors and Terminals function.

The IT Infrastructure Library
Network Services Management

Section 4
Implementation

4. Implementation

This section describes the implementation of the planned Network Services Management function.

4.1 Implementation procedures

The natural order for implementation of the components of the NSM function is:

* implement Network Services Planning (NSP)
* implement Network Services Administration (NSA)
* implement Network Services Control (NSC)
* implement Network Services Project Control (NSPC) (to be activated when necessary)
* assemble the Technical Network Library.

Other general implementation issues are discussed in the rest of this section.

4.1.1 Installation and testing of support tools

NSM support tools must be installed and tested, followed by the rectification of any teething problems. Problems of a minor nature which would not affect the successful operation of the system need not be fixed before the NSM function is implemented. However, a log of such problems should be kept and they should be rectified as soon as is practicable, following implementation.

4.1.2 Training

As soon as the support tools have been installed and are available for use, staff training in their use should be carried out. It may be possible to combine this training with the testing of tools. Staff training in the procedures of the NSM function should also be carried out.

4.1.3 Publicize implementation

The Network Services Manager should publicize the implementation timescales for the new NSM procedures. All people who are affected, in particular users of the network services, IT Services staff and external suppliers and service providers, must be notified and must be reminded of their responsibility to adhere to the new procedures from the outset. The Help Desk should liaise with all users of the network services to keep them informed.

4.1.4 Populate the NDB

The Network Database (NDB) must be populated with all data required for initial operation, and then maintained. If a new or replacement network has been installed, then much of this data should have been captured during installation of the network. Either way, it is essential that all necessary data is captured before the NSM function commences operation.

4.1.5 Finalize reports

The implementation period is also when management reporting styles and layouts are finalized. See section 3.1.8.2 for details of responsibilities for production of reports and recipients of reports. The timing and content of these should be established and agreed well in advance of the implementation date.

4.1.6 Conduct on-going publicity campaign

It is unrealistic to expect that all objectives, across the wide range of aspects covered, will be achieved in less than 9-18 months. The Network Services Manager should carry out an on-going publicity campaign, with a monthly progress sheet, directed at both senior managers and users, as an effective way of ensuring that each benefit of NSM receives publicity as it is achieved.

4.2 Dependencies

Ensure that the plans described in section 3.1 have been implemented and that the dependencies described in section 3.2 have been addressed prior to implementing the NSM function.

IT Management support will be needed to ensure the NSM function obtains the necessary resources and to overcome any resistance from existing service management functions such as Capacity Management and Availability Management.

The success of the NSM function depends on it being adequately resourced. Additional staff may be required for a short period at implementation time (eg to assist with populating the NDB, a task which should not be under estimated).

Section 4
Implementation

4.3 People

The Network Services Manager (or Project Manager if different) is responsible for overseeing the implementation of NSM.

Other personnel requirements are discussed in section 3.3 and throughout the module.

4.4 Timing

For greenfield sites, a core team for NSA and NSC should exist before the implementation of the network commences. The team can be quite small but needs to build up as the implementation progresses.

The full administration and operations team should be in place at least 6 to 12 weeks before a new network is commissioned (ie before the bring into service (BIS) date). This allows enough time for acceptance testing of the new network and associated services to take place. Formal training on the systems and services should precede this period.

It is also useful to select a small core of trial users for implementation testing before the BIS date. This allows NSM to exercise the service management procedures before the network goes live.

The IT Infrastructure Library
Network Services Management

5. Post-implementation and audit

This section covers the review of the Network Services Management project and the procedures for the ongoing review for effectiveness and efficiency of the Network Services Management function. It also covers regular and ad-hoc auditing for compliance to procedures and to the IT Security Policy (to ensure that defined levels of security are both adequate and justifiable).

5.1 Procedures

A project evaluation review (PER) should be conducted as soon as possible after the implementation of NSM is completed, in order to assess the effectiveness of the implementation project. This review is not of direct value to the review of NSM but could provide information about why the function is/is not operating effectively (as may subsequently be detected by the post-implementation review).

A post-implementation review (PIR), conducted about 6/9 months after implementation of NSM, is used to assess the effectiveness of the function, that is the procedures which have been planned and implemented. Regular reviews should follow the PIR in order to ensure that the procedures remain appropriate and effective.

Regular reviews by external staff should take place to ensure continued confidence in the security measures that exist. The reviews could be combined with a regular risk management exercise, using the CCTA Risk Assessment and Management method (CRAMM). Such reviews must be followed up by remedial and improvement actions.

5.1.1 Project evaluation review

The objective of the project evaluation review is to provide an assessment of the management of the project to ensure that the experience gained is documented and used in future projects. It should review:

* actual timescales, resource utilization and the achievement of milestones against planned

* the effectiveness of the management procedures, tools and processes used

* any problems encountered by the project and how they were, and with hindsight should have been, resolved.

5.1.2 Post-implementation review

It is recommended that a formal post-implementation review, which could represent the final phase of the development project, is conducted about 6 to 9 months after the full network services management function is put into operation.

The IT Services Manager is responsible for initiating the first post-implementation review, to be carried out by an independent reviewer.

The purpose of the review is to assess how well the objectives of the NSM function are being met (see section 3.1.3). The review should check indicators for an effective network services management function, which include:

* are SLAs breached because of poor network service quality?

* are improvements in service quality which can be attributed to improvements to the network service realized?

* are there defined objectives for network service performance?

* do performance levels meet objectives?

* has network service availability improved since the implementation of the new/improved function?

* are any reasonable demands for network capacity not anticipated?

* (if users receive network services directly) - what are users' opinions on the services provided?

* when was the last time an accurate survey of users' opinions was undertaken?

* are costs within budget, are they accurately tracked, managed and allocated?

* how close is the cost profile to the planned budgets?

* do changes to the network and/or services result in any incidents or problems?

* is the Technical Network Library complete, up-to-date and a back-up copy stored off-site?

* are responsibilities for changes to the network clearly identified, documented and adhered to?

Section 5
Post-implementation and audit

* are there documented and fully tested contingency plans available for inspection?
* have the procedures for backing-up configurations been adhered to?
* has the organization's and/or network IT Security Policy been adhered to?
* are IT and business management provided with regular reports and reviews on network services targets?

It is imperative that the necessary monitoring and control activities are designed into all basic procedures and practices in order for network services management to be able to answer these questions. Control over costs, quality and risks is not possible without adequate management information.

5.1.3 Ongoing operation and review

The day-to-day operation of NSM covers many of the functions listed in section 5.1.2. Reviews of the ongoing operation should check that:

* tasks required to manage the network services are being performed
* the network service is satisfactory to the business and operates within time and budget constraints.

Annex B contains lists which may be used to review whether tasks are being performed.

5.1.4 Reviewing for efficiency and effectiveness

Many of the issues discussed in section 5.1.2 under the post-implementation review apply equally to regular efficiency and effectiveness reviews, which are intended to show that the procedures and practices of NSM deliver a quality network service. Periodic reviews can be held to ensure that:

* the benefits of NSM are being delivered efficiently and effectively
* shortcomings in the function are identified and corrected at the earliest possible date
* the function is well managed by the Network Services Manager

* possible improvements to the NSM function are identified, and carried out if cost-justified.

The main questions for an efficiency and effectiveness review of the NSM function are:

* does senior management accept and implement the Network Services Manager's recommendations? (Investigate the effectiveness of communication, verify that IT Service Managers understand the rôle of Network Services Management in the long-term provision of IT services)

* are the network services satisfactory to the customers and are service levels met? (Examine the understanding of the configuration and incidents and the procedures used to rectify breaches in service levels)

* do enhancements and upgrades to the network cause problems?

* could the NSM function be improved? (Investigate contribution of activities to objectives, effectiveness of procedures and use of support tools; encourage staff suggestions - the people who work in the area often know how procedures could be improved)

* have the performance claims of suppliers and manufacturers been checked against contract conditions?

* does the NSM function produce the right information, at the right time, in the right format, for the right people? (Investigate the satisfaction with provided reports and changes in the need for reports).

Reviews should be carried out by the Network Services Manager at least every twelve months. It is recommended that the IT Services Manager annually initiates a formal review. The Network Services Manager should produce and implement plans, based on information obtained during a review, to rectify any shortcomings. Reviews should be aligned and streamlined with similar reviews in other IT infrastructure management functions, such as Configuration Management, Problem Management, Capacity Management and Availability Management.

Consideration should be given to the use of services such as Decision Support Centre (DSC) from ACT Business Systems. DSC provides a detailed analysis and assessment of the IT services organization's performance relative to

Section 5
Post-implementation and audit

similar organizations and can identify areas for improvement. DSC has specific services for data & voice networks and distributed systems. Such services may also provide evidence of the potential benefits of outsourcing (or, indeed, of continued insourcing).

5.1.5 Auditing for compliance

The following checklist can be used to audit NSM for compliance to the procedures and advice in this module. It is recommended that an audit is completed at least annually. It is also recommended that such audits are performed by either the organization's computer audit section, which is independent of IT Services, or by an external organization.

The audit of NSM should check that:

* the communication of NSM with all relevant IT service management functions takes place and is effective

* reviews of NSM are carried out regularly as planned

* all requests for change (RFCs) affecting the network are assessed by the NSM function

* all necessary reports are produced and published according to the agreed schedules

* the Technical Network Library is complete, up-to-date and that a back-up copy is stored off-site

* data held in the Network Database (NDB) is consistent with that held in the Configuration Management Database (CMDB), where these are physically separate, and is accurate

* network services are determined from, and reflect services specified in, the Service Catalogue

* the IT Security Policy is followed

* all responsibilities and rôles are clearly defined and adhered to.

5.2 Dependencies

The dependencies listed in sections 3.2 and 4.2 are also applicable to the ongoing operations of the Network Services Management function. The most important dependencies are:

* continued commitment to NSM by senior management

* the desire to improve continually the service to business (once more, cost must be balanced against quality)

* the integration of network services and computer operations management, particularly where systems are being or have been de-centralized.

5.3 People

The Network Services Manager has overall responsibility for the running of NSM.

The IT Services Manager or IT Director should arrange for periodic audits of Network Services Management by independent computer audit teams. Such audits should complement the audits and reviews which are a feature of a quality IT service.

Annual reviews should also check:

* the number of staff and appropriate skill levels required to support the functions identified as necessary (particularly important given the rapid advancements which are being made in automated tools)

* whether the organizational structure is appropriate for the needs of the business

* whether the organizational structure is appropriate for the type of IT system being supported, given the move away from centralized systems.

Training

The training programme should be maintained and re-assessed through regular reviews of training needs.

In order to broaden the knowledge and skills of NSM staff it may be beneficial to arrange for staff to be seconded to other areas (where they exist separately) such as Capacity Management, Availability Management and Configuration Management.

A natural career progression is from NSC to NSA, then to NSP, finally Network Services Manager, each function drawing on experience and expertise gained in the previous posting.

Section 5
Post-implementation and audit

5.4 Timing

PER	The project evaluation review should take place as soon as possible after the implementation of NSM is completed.
Regular reviews	The operational activities required after the implementation are continuous. It is important, therefore, to have regular audits and reviews to check the status of the installation and the underlying trends that exist. These audits and reviews should be undertaken typically every twelve months, and should be timed to allow for any necessary expenditure to be included in the plans for the next financial year.
PIR	In particular, a post-implementation review should be carried out between six and nine months after implementation of NSM or any major network implementation or enhancement.
Alignment	Reviews should be aligned with similar reviews in other IT infrastructure management functions such as Configuration Management, Problem Management, Capacity Management and Availability Management.
Demonstrable success	The time taken to introduce and establish the practices recommended in this module should not be underestimated. It is unrealistic to expect that demonstrable success, across the wide range of aspects covered, will be achieved in less than nine to eighteen months. Despite this, it is valuable to look for early benefits such as improved customer satisfaction or cost savings through the use of automated tools.
	Implementation of Configuration and Change Management functions is most likely to reap early benefits although, in the absence of existing functions, it is unlikely that the necessary metrics will exist for objective measurement of improvements.

The IT Infrastructure Library
Network Services Management

Section 6
Benefits, costs and possible problems

6. Benefits, costs and possible problems

This section outlines the benefits and costs of implementing Network Services Management and points out some of the potential problems that should be avoided.

The problems involved in managing network services are a microcosm of the problems that exist in the overall IT infrastructure. Consequently, the issues to be resolved are part of the overall problems facing the IT organization and many of the costs, risks and benefits are the same.

6.1 Benefits

6.1.1 Benefits to the business

The business benefit stemming from effective Network Services Management is the reliable and consistent matching of network services to user needs (ie **service quality**), which, in turn, contributes to the overall success of the organization's business through higher productivity. This benefit is achieved through:

* increased service availability to users
* capacity matched to users' requirements
* less adverse impact of changes on the quality of IT services, because changes are carefully controlled
* more efficient handling of problems
* lower costs of IT service provision (through the benefits to IT Services)
* reducing risk of network failure and minimization of the effect of such failure.

6.1.2 Benefits to IT Services

Network Services Management helps IT Services become more efficient and effective by:

* managing changes to network hardware and software - reducing the resources needed to cope with the adverse effects of changes
* managing problems - monitoring network service levels enables trends and problems to be identified quickly and dealt with, reducing the resources required to handle problems; analysing the cause of problems helps to reduce the number of problems

The IT Infrastructure Library
Network Services Management

* anticipating problems - potential performance, capacity, and availability problems can be anticipated, and corrective action instigated to prevent a crisis

* helping the IT directorate to understand their network infrastructures, leading to more informed decisions

* increased productivity of key IT personnel (less fire-fighting)

* reducing risk of not meeting commitments

* identifying new technology which can save costs and/or improve service levels

* planning expansions and upgrades - by maintaining a close match between demand and capacity the organization makes efficient use of resources.

6.2 Costs

The costs of implementing a NSM function are:

* staff recruitment, training and salaries - for all responsibilities falling within the scope of NSM

* accommodation for staff and equipment - including accommodation for third party staff who are required to be on-site either on a permanent or temporary basis

* tools, including hardware, software and associated training costs - these should be balanced against savings in staff time.

6.3 Possible problems

Communication	There is a need to interface and communicate with many other IT Services staff. Problems can arise if such communication either does not take place or is not effective.
Cultural change	In most organizations, the introduction of new or modified procedures involves a significant cultural change. There are inherent limits to the rapidity with which this can be achieved.
Skilled staff	Difficulty might be encountered due to the lack of suitably skilled staff. This can be overcome by selecting a core team for the overall project and instigating a training programme to supplement existing skills and experience, before the project starts. External assistance may need to be sought for specialist skills, thereby adding to the costs.

Section 6
Benefits, costs and possible problems

Lack of money — Even if the benefits of effectively managed network services are accepted, there may not be sufficient funds to implement the necessary changes. In such a climate, an incremental approach will be the only feasible means of progressing, with the benefits of each increment supporting the justification for the next phase. The phases should therefore be prioritized to give early, large and visible returns.

Availability of technology — The existing network and management systems may not be able to provide enough of the functionality and information required to manage the network and services effectively. This is true both in terms of the command, control and configuration level of functionality as well as information on, for example, performance and usage.

Lock-in to existing technology — If the network and/or management systems are proprietary (and without the necessary standard protocols and interfaces), then the technology availability problem will be compounded because the number of alternative solutions will be limited.

The problem could be overcome by augmenting the current network and management systems with additional software. However, this is often an expensive approach (in the longer term) and should be regarded as a short-term solution. It is better to ensure that a technology replacement policy is included in the organization's IT Strategy/Infrastructure Plan, which enables the organization to obtain the control, functionality and management information that it needs in the longer term.

Perception — The rapid growth of networking and the penetration of IT (particularly LANs and PCs) into mainstream business activities may lead some senior managers to doubt (because of the relative cheapness of individual components) the necessity for the breadth and depth of activities covered in this module and for the support tools required. The perception may be that IT is just office equipment rather than a sophisticated system which requires careful management in order to deliver the potential benefits.

Standards — There are as yet (1994) no comprehensive de-jure international or national (UK) standards for network management (see annex F for further discussion). Network management standards are developing fast but it will probably be several years before the full benefits of truly integrated network management and systems management are achieved. However with careful selection of tools and protocols (effectively creating in-house standards) many benefits can be achieved even without comprehensive de-jure standards.

Availability of tools	There are many tools available which address different aspects of network management (see section 7 and annex E), but few tools provide much integration, particularly with those used for other service management functions. Unfortunately, those which do are generally proprietary, and therefore require the use of proprietary network hardware and/or software. However, by careful selection and planning a viable set of tools can be used to help meet current needs until better solutions become available (see prior paragraph on standards).
	It is unlikely that a single supplier will be able to meet all an organization's Network Services Management needs, either now or in the future. In future the development of a detailed and wide ranging set of inter-operability standards for management purposes may make it easier to obtain integrated tool sets. Even then, however, suppliers are likely to add non-standard functionality to differentiate their products from others.
	In addition, given the increased availability of managed and virtual network services it is unlikely that such service providers will allow external management systems to fully interact with the control and configuration of the network services they provide. This will always lead to multiple network support tools being required.
Security of management tools	Network management tools, by providing a high level of access across the network, introduce a security risk. This may be exacerbated by the use of protocols (such as SNMP) with no inherent security. This problem will become more manageable as protocols and tools mature. In the meantime, where the level of risk justifies it, careful control and monitoring of the use of management tools will be required, together with more stringent control over physical access to the network.

7. Tools

7.1 Introduction

The majority of tools currently available for NSM have developed from a bottom up approach to network management systems (NMS), ie many have evolved from basic test equipment or configuration utilities. The functionality of these systems has been enhanced and integrated with other supporting systems, such as performance monitoring systems, to form the current product offerings of many vendors.

There has been considerable interest in NSM tools from Network Services Managers. This has been motivated by the hope that these tools will reduce both the complexity inherent in large, multi-vendor network environments and the resource requirements needed to support them. If the capabilities of the management tools cannot be developed at the same rate of growth as the size and complexity of the networks, more and more effort and personnel will be required to perform the NSM functions.

Network management has developed a long way since the early data communications networks of the sixties and seventies, where network management was either dumb terminal system or a 'black box', with very limited user/operator interface, and even more limited functionality. The inter-working networks of the nineties require more than just ad- hoc network management. They require total NSM functionality, which consists of more than just network management systems (NMS) and technical support tools. It can be thought of as the four supporting disciplines, each requiring a set of tools, enabling them to complete their job. These tools must be inter-connected, and exchange data in a compatible and consistent format, for NSM to function efficiently as part of the NSM 7 Layer model:

* Network Services Planning (NSP) require tools to assist with the long-term strategic networking issues, especially those of network design and planning

* Network Services Administration (NSA) need short-term tactical networking tools to assist with their tasks of network data collection, analysis and reporting

* Network Services Control (NSC) require operational tools for the purposes of immediate decision making on the day-to-day operational aspects of the network

> * Network Services Planning Control (NSPC) require tools to assist with the management and control of major network implementation projects.

These four disciplines need to be fully integrated in their operations, allowing the Network Services Manager to fully support the total network service.

The rest of this section is organized thus:

> * a description of network management systems (7.2)
>
> * a discussion of the general requirement for NSM tools (7.3)
>
> * guidance on selecting tools (7.4)
>
> * a brief description of interface requirements for tools (7.5)
>
> * an overview of current tools (7.6, detail in annex E)
>
> * advantages and pitfalls of using tools for NSM (7.7)
>
> * a simple summary of the route towards integration (7.8).

7.2 Network management systems (NMSs)

The principal tool of the NSM function is the system management tool or network management system. There are many different NMSs offering many and varied facilities, so it is essential that a system with the required functionality is selected. NMSs are by design either proprietary or non-proprietary in their operation and support, although hybrid systems do exist.

7.2.1 The proprietary approach to NMSs

To provide an integrated view of the network requires the standardization of the definition and structure of data between networks, and for network components to be represented by events (for behaviour) and objects (for static properties). However, as many of the current generation of systems have developed from basic configuration control and test systems, each discrete proprietary NMS holds data in a dissimilar way. The interfaces to such systems and the structure of this data are often deemed to be commercially confidential information, with most suppliers unwilling to release this information to others.

The situation is further complicated by the lack of control over the definition and structure of this data between version releases of the systems. Even if the detail of the data is released it would require a continuous development effort to track the changes to it. This is neither practical nor economic.

This situation prevents Network Services Managers from developing an integrated, end-to-end view of the overall network. They are forced by necessity to have different NMSs for each set of network elements used in the network structure, often leading to a situation where different systems exist for:

* modem management
* PBX management
* Kilostream multiplexor management
* Megastream multiplexor management
* LAN management
* WAN management
* network performance monitoring.

In some cases, there can be two or three systems managing the same type of network element, eg modems, if each group of modems has been purchased from different suppliers. This means that separate management domains develop, each managed by its own NMS, as shown in figure 10.

This situation is undesirable and the organization needs to develop a strategy for moving towards an integrated NMS based on standards.

7.2.2 The non-proprietary approach to NMSs

A non-proprietary solution to integrating network management systems requires a standardized approach to be adopted.

Network management standards are primarily centred on protocols for the communication of management data - that is the properties and behaviour of network elements - illustrated on layer 2 of the NSM 7-layer model in figure 13 overleaf.

There are two basic facts to recognize before considering network management standards:

* if a device does not support the network management protocol selected you cannot manage the device

* if the network being used does not allow the network management protocol to pass, you cannot manage the network.

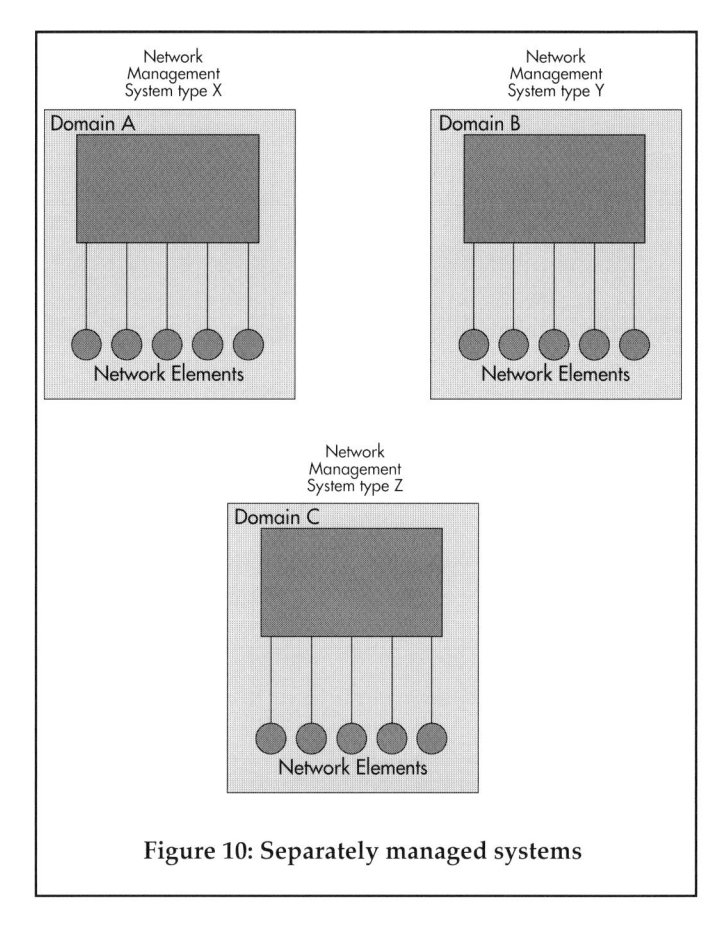

Figure 10: Separately managed systems

There are seven major sets of network management standards available for use today:

Distributed Management Environment (DME)
This is a set of standards, defined by the Open Software Foundation (OSF), that supply technology implementations for distributed systems management. It provides a basis for a comprehensive, consistent system administration and network management platform.

UK GOSIP
These are UK Government standards, relating to network management, which refer to a recommended set of standards to be used for network management. Eventually they will consist of an integrated set of sub-profiles, but as an intercept standard at the moment they refer to the OSI Common Management Information Protocol (CMIP) and the Common Management Information Service (CMIS).

OMNI*Point*	This is a set of standards defined by the Network Management Forum (NMF). A number of the major network user organizations and network suppliers have established the OSI Network Management Forum (NMF), in an attempt to develop working network management standards in advance of the OSI standards. This has given rise to another set of working network management standards and products.
Open Systems Interconnection (OSI)	OSI management systems use the Common Management Information Protocol (CMIP), although there are comparatively few products and systems as yet supporting this protocol. However it is seen by many as the way forward for NMSs of the future. The full set of OSI network management protocols will probably be developed over the next three or four years.
System Network Architecture (SNA)	NMSs based on the proprietary Systems Network Architecture (SNA) are almost exclusively used by the IBM Netview range of products for the control of IBM networks. There are also non-IBM products that now support the Netview standards.
Telecommunications Network Model	This is a ITU/TS (formerly CCITT) standard used in the telecommunications industry as a model to achieve coordination between operations support systems and network switching technology. It has been incorporated into the OMNI*Point* series and is a subset of the NMF's OMNI*Point* standards.
Transmission Control Protocol/Internet Protocol (TCP/IP) Environments	NMSs which manage TCP/IP environments utilize the Simple Network Management Protocol (SNMP) which in turn uses the TCP/IP transmission protocol suite developed initially by the Department of Defence in the USA and controlled by the Internet Advisory Board (IAB). These systems are generally used for the management of LANs and LAN products. Most network equipment suppliers produce NMSs based on SNMP and it is probably the most commonly used system for network management.
Which one to choose?	More information on the major standards and their capabilities can be found in annex F.
	TCP/IP and SNMP offer a comparatively restricted set of network management facilities, but have become widely used because of their inclusion within Unix systems. IBM's Netview and SNA systems are proprietary and are therefore used only for the management of IBM networks although some network equipment suppliers do provide Netview

interfaces. Mixing management protocols (on separate segments) is theoretically possible, but requires very careful tool selection - a management tool which accepts both protocols is required. The Network Management Forum's Open Management Edge enables this mixing of management protocols to some degree (see section 7.2.3). However the strategic, long-term, way forward for NMSs is using the OSI network management protocols, which will give full functionality using internationally agreed standards.

7.2.3 The integrated approach to NMSs

The majority of the above standards introduce the concept of managers, agents and managed objects to network management. This engineering approach allows NMSs to be inter-connected to form a single enterprise-wide network management system. An example of this integration (between domains A and B) is displayed in figure 11. Domain C remains stand-alone because its NMS is incompatible.

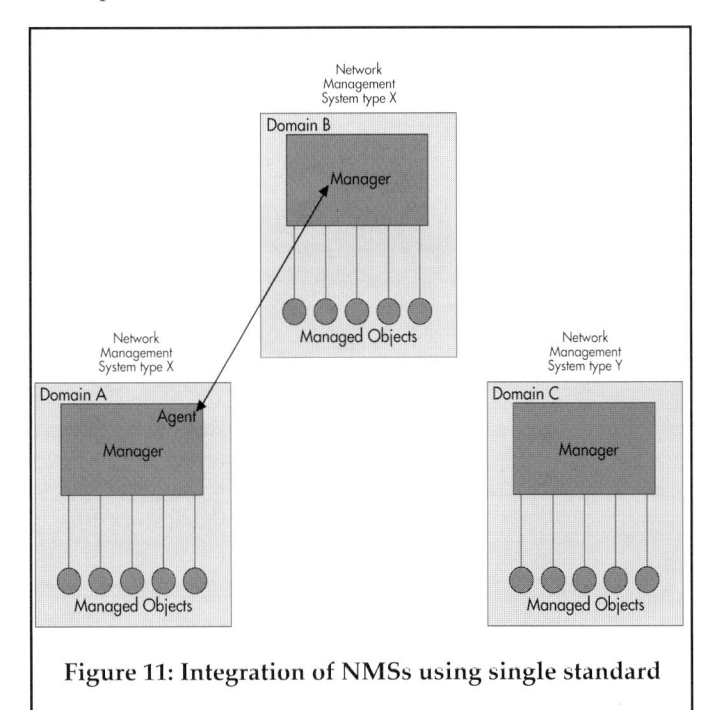

Figure 11: Integration of NMSs using single standard

However in reality this is very difficult to achieve, and ignores the problem of legacy systems, that is existing systems which do not conform to any particular standard.

Section 7
Tools

The NMF have further developed this concept and, with their OMNI*Point* programme, demonstrated the inter-working of different NMSs. Stage 1 of this programme (OMNI*Point* 1) introduced the concept of the 'Open Management Edge' which facilitates the exchange of information between NMSs from different network suppliers. The Edge Request Broker (ERB) serves as a broker which allows managed and management systems to register an interest in the types of messages (ie management protocol) that they wish to receive. An example of this integration (between domains A and B) is displayed in figure 12. By adding a service link module to domain C, it would be able to communicate with domains A and B via a common protocol.

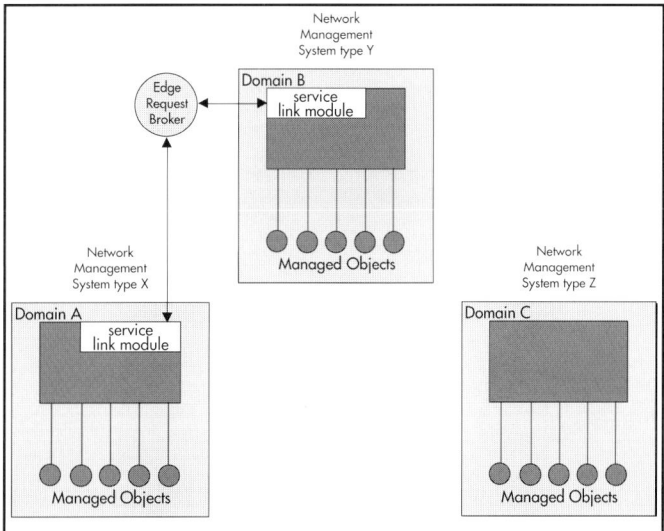

Figure 12: Partial integration of different NMSs using the "Open Management Edge"

This concept is not limited to the inter-working of NMSs, but can be applied to any management system, it could for instance be implemented within a Configuration Management system, or indeed any other Service Management tool. Once 'the edge' has been implemented, a single physical network connection can be used to connect to any number of other management systems and exchange data in a standard format. This points the way forward for the development of a comprehensive, integrated NSM function, which then fulfils the business requirements of the organization. It encourages the production of a set of fully integrated IT and NSM tools providing full NSM functionality. More details on these network management standards can be found in annex F.

7.3 Tool requirement

7.3.1 Functional requirements

Management of a network consists of more than just an NMS. It comprises an integrated set of NSM tools fulfilling the requirements of the four disciplines that underpin the operation of the NSM function. The tools themselves provide the scope of layer 3 of the NSM model, but they must satisfy the needs of layers 4, 5, 6 and 7. The tools required for each of the functions are:

* **Network Services Planning** requires tools to assist with the long-term strategic networking issues. NSP need tools to assist with the following functions

    - establishing and reporting on trends

    - planning and decision making

    - all aspects of Capacity and Availability Planning

    - network design and optimization

    - network costing

    - network disaster recovery

    - establishing requirements and evaluating alternative solutions.

* **Network Services Administration** needs short-term tactical networking tools to assist with the following tasks

    - network SLA monitoring and exception reporting

    - network accounting and charging

    - network Configuration Management

    - network Software Control and Distribution

    - identification of network bottlenecks and potential bottlenecks

    - reporting on usage trends

    - network Change Management

    - network security monitoring and control

    - planning and decision making

    - preparation of procedures for NSC

    - analysis of incidents and problems

Section 7
Tools

* **Network Services Control** requires operational tools for the purposes of immediate decision making on the day-to-day operational aspects of the network

    - interpreting network events and alarms
    - network operation and control
    - network equipment reload and recovery
    - incident recording and problem determination and control
    - collection and storage of data on service and performance levels
    - equipment configuration maintenance
    - activation/deactivation of network components
    - proactive preventative maintenance
    - network testing and monitoring
    - automating procedures

* **Network Services Project Control** requires tools to assist with the management and control of implementation projects

    - project management and control
    - network implementation, stress testing, pilot testing
    - network software distribution and control.

All of the NSM functions will also need reasonable access to office automation equipment and services, principally database tools, diary systems, word processors, graphical systems, statistical analysis packages, spreadsheets and E-mail systems. Each organization should have its own recommended set of office automation tools, such that standard analysis models and reports can be produced. Wherever possible these systems should be integrated with all of the other systems in use within NSM, with automatic procedures being used as much as possible to facilitate the exchange of data.

In order to achieve complete integration between the tools and the disciplines, a layered approach to NSM must be adopted by the Network Services Manager:

The IT Infrastructure Library
Network Services Management

7 Business Management Accounting/Billing/Design/Development/ Operations/Planning & Control...
6 Network Services Management Configuration Control/Cost Management/ Enhancement Programmes/Fault Management/ Quality of Service/Resource Optimization/Security Control
5 NSM Supporting Disciplines NSP/NSA/NSC/NSPC
4 NSM Mechanisms Configuration Maintainance/Data Collection/ Diagnostic Monitoring and Testing/Fault Detection /Operation and Control/Project Planning/ Performance Monitoring/Report Production/Statistical Analysis...
3 NSM Tools Capacity Management/Costing/Databases/ Environmental Monitoring/Modelling/Office Automation/ Project Management/Planning and Design/Service Management/Service Monitoring/ Statistical Analysis/Systems Management/Testing...
2 Network Management Standards OSI/GOSIP MGT/OMNIpoint/TCP/IP(SNMP)...
1 Network Technology LANs/MANs/WANs/Voice/ISDN...

Figure 13: NSM 7-layer model

Security   Security is a particular requirement of all NSM tools. Management tools do, in general, give their users the ability to compromise the security of the network. For instance, the SNMP protocol allows any user to re-configure the network; network analysers may allow data blocks to be intercepted and read, or even modified.

Section 7
Tools

7.3.2 Tool categories

The tools used to provide the functionality of layer 3 of the mode, fall into a number of different categories, and each may provide support for some or all of the requirements of the supporting disciplines of NSM.

7.3.2.1 Network management systems (NMSs)

Network management systems provide the day-to-day monitoring, control and coordination of the managed network components within their domain. Many different types of network management systems exist for the management of different components. The three major types of network management systems, together with the facilities they should provide are data network management, voice management and cable management.

Data network management

Most existing tools are proprietary in nature, although some use SNMP and some support interfaces to other network management software. Almost all of the major LAN and WAN equipment suppliers can provide proprietary NMSs for their own products and manage other manufacturer's equipment using the SNMP protocol. Recently products have begun to emerge that support the OMNI*Point* standards and can exchange network information in a compatible and consistent format.

The facilities that should be supported by data NMSs are as follows:

* handling of events, warnings and alarms of different priorities
* multiple levels of management access control
* local and remote configuration of components
* download and upload of equipment configurations
* download and upload of equipment software
* unit, component, board, port and link reload/reset
* monitoring of physical level interfaces
* traffic monitoring and statistics
* accounting and billing facilities
* traffic balancing
* performance and availability monitoring
* diagnostics tracing facilities

The IT Infrastructure Library
Network Services Management

* alternate re-routeing in the event of failure
* isolation of failed network areas
* traffic filtering and security
* multi-layer graphical network representations
* graphical display and control down to individual circuit board level
* central network log and audit trail
* security control and service access facilities
* security monitoring facilities
* unit, component, port and link status interrogation
* application of loop tests and test pattern generation
* a component database with interfaces to other tools
* database dump and recovery procedures
* data analysis and reporting facilities
* timer initiated activities
* user configurable and scripting facilities
* user configurable threshold and trigger alarms
* interfaces to other NSM tools.

Voice management

Voice management systems, sometimes referred to as 'traffic management systems' or 'call management systems', assist with the monitoring of calls made through Private Branch Exchanges (PBXs) and switches. Most traffic or call management system will identify the traffic flows internally through the switch and also calls in and out of the switch to the public network or other linked PBXs. Some systems also offer command, configuration and control facilities for the locally connected PBX and also remotely connected PBXs.

The management systems vary from simple call recorders to Call Information Logging Equipment (CILE) through to full systems management. The most sophisticated systems are now known as Switch Management Systems. These systems may be used to predict the growth of the voice network and its bottle-necks. Typical facilities provided by the more sophisticated systems include:

* handling of events, warnings and alarms of different priorities
* multiple levels of management access control

Section 7
Tools

* local and remote configuration of components
* download and upload of equipment configurations
* collection of call duration and volume statistics
* traffic balancing
* alternate re-routeing in the event of failure
* multi-layer graphical network representations
* graphical component control down to board level
* central network log and audit trail
* security control and service access facilities
* unit/component status
* a component database with interfaces to other tools
* reporting facilities
* interfaces to other NSM tools.

Cable management Tools for cable management are available in essentially two types. The first is an automated database, and the second links this type of database to a Computer Aided Design (CAD) facility. The functionality of the systems will vary but should consist of:

* recording cable number, position (from/to), type, length, installer, route, date, status, equipment connected
* automatic production of cable schedules for purchasing purposes
* automatic production of labels
* component database
* alerts for cable route overload
* alerts if maximum cable lengths are exceeded
* geographic representation of circuits/patching
* interface with integrated CAD system
* a component database with interfaces to other tools
* reporting facilities
* interfaces to other NSM tools.

Some cable management systems also provide computer controlled patching (ie line connection) facility, thereby obviating the need for physical patch moves. This can obviously save time, particularly in fall-back situations, as alternative configurations can be prepared in advance. For more information see the **Specification and Management of a Cable Infrastructure** module.

7.3.2.2 Network services software

Network services software may, by design, provide the following useful features:

* network transaction response times

* information on transaction processing and queuing times

* security and access control to areas of the network service

* transaction statistics ie types, sizes and volumes

* transaction audit trail facilities

* transaction control and management

* download of software to remote equipment

* tracing and diagnostic logs

* configuration and re-configuration of operational parameters

* code translation

* protocol conversion

* alternate routeing

* activation and de-activation of components

* reporting facilities

* interfaces to other NSM tools.

These features may be provided by the native operating system of the host system, system software or application software.

7.3.2.3 Network testing tools

Network testing tools of many different types and sophistication exist, and can be used for a multitude of purposes from problem diagnosis to network simulation and planning. The following are some of the more common tools.

Break out boxes/ interface testers
These are generally very cheap testers but are essential for first line problem diagnosis. They are available for many different physical interfaces and some of the more expensive sets provide quite sophisticated testing facilities:

* interface signal patching and monitoring
* Bit Error Rate Testing (BERT)
* equipment functional tests.

Circuit and cable testers
These are generally fairly cheap but useful tools for first line problem diagnosis. They are available for many different physical interfaces and provide good testing facilities:

* continuity tests
* cable connection tests.

Media scanners
These vary in complexity and cost but are essential tools to ensure that the quality of the cable installation is within standard and specification. These tools have facilities for:

* media quality tests
* media specification tests
* reporting facilities.

Network monitors/ analysers and remote probes
Network monitors/analysers can either be PCs with specialized hardware and software or may be purpose built pieces of equipment. However they should provide the following facilities:

* protocol decode and analysis
* traffic statistics
* traffic generators
* reflect tests
* timing tests
* line monitoring
* problem determination
* error testing and analysis

* variety of physical interface simulation/monitoring

* reporting facilities.

These tools vary in their complexity, functionality and cost. They may vary from analogue and digital transmission analysers to sophisticated LAN protocol analysers or hybrid analysers with dual functionality. These tools are more than pure test and diagnostic aids. They can form an integral part of the network Capacity Management function, because of their ability to record and analyse performance information. It is because of this ability that some of these tools have developed into remote portable online diagnostics (PODS), probes or Management Information Bases (MIBs). Some of the original MIBs were proprietary but standard specifications exist for MIBs both in the OSI and SNMP network management standards and these are now becoming more readily available. These purpose built devices can remain permanently connected to the network at strategic points and be left to accumulate performance information and provide useful information to the network Capacity Management function. However, if left connected, appropriate security measures will be necessary in order to avoid disclosure of passwords and other sensitive information.

7.3.2.4 Network planning/design tools

This category of tools is used to assist with the network design and planning process. In conjunction with modelling techniques (see 7.3.2.5), these tools allow the network planner to plan a network which will meet the business requirements by evaluating different protocols, technologies and topologies. The following features may be supported:

* graphical network interface

* LAN technologies (Ethernet, Token Ring etc.)

* WAN technologies (X25, SNA, ATM etc.)

* libraries of LAN components (ie bridges, routers etc.)

* libraries of WAN components (ie circuit/packet switches)

* libraries of link protocols

* libraries of routeing algorithms

* evaluation of 'what if' scenarios

* interfaces to network Capacity Management

* facilities for defining customized objects
* report generation facilities.

Simulation tools and techniques can be expensive in terms of the resources used, however provided that the input information is correct the results obtained can prove accurate and often impossible to obtain any other way. The traffic generator tools mentioned in section 7.3.2.5 can also be used in the network planning/design process.

The NDB may also contain information used for capacity management (typically held in a separate Capacity Management Database for host computer capacity management). It tends to be rather more complex since it includes geographic and circuit costing information in addition to performance statistics, service level data and technical equipment criteria. Subsets of the information are used in all areas of network management, for example for voice and data network planning and installation, configuration management, performance analysis, Help Desk information and billing.

7.3.2.5 Network capacity management tools

These may be required by NSM, but some or all of them may already be in use within the Capacity Management function. If a separate Capacity Management function does not exist then the tools will have to be obtained. There are five separate categories of network capacity management tools.

Network Database (NDB) — Tools are required to accumulate and manipulate the NDB. The NDB should exist as part of the overall Capacity Management Database (CDB) wherever possible under the control of the Capacity Management function. The NDB should have facilities to:

* manipulate the data through a standard interface (such as SQL if it is a relational database management system)
* archive old data
* import and export data from/to network management systems through standard protocols such as SNMP and CMIP
* import and export data from/to service management tools and databases through standard protocols such as SQL or SNMP and CMIP
* analyse statistics

	* display information graphically
	* allow room for growth.
Network performance monitoring	Mechanisms for performance monitoring often exist within system management tools and network testing tools, some of which already have in-built data import and export facilities. Also some of the network service software can provide useful performance monitoring facilities. Other useful sources of performance data can be test Management Information Bases (MIBs) which can be left to collect information and then polled to extract the stored information from them. Priorities between testing requirements and performance monitoring activities will have to be determined as conflicts in demands for a shared resource will occur, unless units are acquired for both needs. Once the information has been captured it should all be loaded into the NDB, preferably automatically. The aspects of the network that need to be monitored are:
	* message sizes and volumes
	* message response times
	* numbers of errors and retransmissions
	* network node loadings and utilizations
	* queue lengths
	* link loadings and utilizations
	* major nodal conversations
	* numbers and durations of connections
	* hunt group utilizations.
	Peak and average statistics should be recorded for all of the performance items above. These figures should not be viewed in isolation but should be used in conjunction with the total information obtained from the host network services, that is why it is imperative that network Capacity Management is run as an integral part of the overall Capacity Management function.
Network modelling	For most purposes PC-based tools are the most suitable for the modelling of networks. However some larger networks may require the use of mini or even mainframe systems. The cost involved in the use of modelling tools can vary considerably, so the use of them must be carefully considered and cost justified. Although they can be expensive, the benefits of using modelling techniques can be enormous and yield results that are impossible to reach

Section 7
Tools

any other way. There are four major types of modelling techniques used: trend analysis, analytical modelling, simulation modelling and traffic generation

Trend analysis

This involves analysing and storing historical data, and building trends in growth of particular facets of the network. The tools most commonly used for this purpose are:

* statistical analysis packages
* spreadsheet packages.

Analytical modelling

Analytical modelling tools generally use mathematical models based on multi-class network queuing theory. They are less expensive to run than simulation tools and the models are much easier to build. They are generally less accurate, but are accurate enough for most purposes. The modelling tools should provide:

* easily configurable models
* graphical output facilities
* flexible reporting.

A trade-off always exists between the main design parameters. Changing any particular parameter alters one or more of the others. When modelling a network it must be decided which parameter is to be optimized:

* the network links
* the networked devices
* the overall performance of the network, eg response times
* the cost profiles for differing topologies
* the network capacity
* network reliability and availability.

The main parameters which are usually chosen for optimization are performance, capacity and reliability/resilience. These must be maximized within the constraints of cost and the service level requirements for the project.

Analytical modelling is useful for establishing the sensitivity of the network parameters to changes in the network structure. It is important to understand and be aware of the limitations of the proposed structure for capacity planning purposes - for instance, would removal of a link severely restrict the capacity of the network or could alternative routes soak up the extra traffic?

The limitation of analytical modelling is that the prediction process is based on an algorithm derived from theory and modified empirically. This means that a real network must already exist, from which measurements are taken, in order to build the model. The algorithm is an approximation of the real network and attempts to predict the traffic flow characteristics; therefore it is essential that the model is calibrated to ensure that it accurately reflects the real situation. The accuracy of the model depends upon the algorithm used, but simulation of the network overcomes this limitation.

Simulation modelling

Simulation is the process whereby known characteristics of a network and its components are built into a computer model of the network structure. The structure then has computer simulated traffic applied to it and the resultant performance analysed.

The advantages of simulation over analytical modelling are that:

* the accuracy of the parameters used to model the network service and system components is greatly increased

* the computer reproduction of the network and systems has 'real' traffic applied to it and the results obtained should be very similar to those obtained in reality.

These advantages allow the network designer considerable benefits by being able to prove each aspect of the design in advance of implementation. This can be done before incurring expenditure on circuits or systems which may not be required. It is often necessary, however, to measure the characteristics of actual systems and circuits, usually via a small test bed of the proposed final system. An alternative source for this information is the network supplier.

A simulation model provides an ideal tool for subsequent Capacity Management and Availability Management purposes. Planned changes, enhancements and failures within the network can be tested during simulation. This can be used to demonstrate that the required network performance or resilience will be met and that the network can carry the modified load.

Section 7
Tools

However, there are disadvantages with simulation. The major disadvantage is the time, effort, expertise, and therefore cost, needed to build and run the simulation. The investment in a representative test bed of the proposed network can be a significant cost overhead. This can however be obviated by validating the simulation using a similar network and equipment at a reference site. Simulation models should always be calibrated against the real network.

Further advances in microcomputer technology, both in effective processing speed and in storage space, are expected to reduce the cost associated with simulation. The use of simulation, particularly in network Capacity Management, is recommended whenever possible, however there may be cases where analytical modelling is a more feasible approach.

The simulation tools need to be:

* easy to use
* have extensive libraries of network components
* have graphical output facilities
* provide flexible reporting.

For more information on Analytical Modelling & Simulation see the **Capacity Management** module.

Traffic generation

Traffic generators may be used to predict the effect of changes to the existing network. These generators come in the form of either hardware, software, or a combination of both. The traffic generation process involves loading an existing area of the network, or network under test, with pseudo-traffic (usually terminal traffic). Analysis of performance and response time changes, to either users or services, can then be conducted using the same monitoring hardware and software, or the usual performance analysis tools. The process may be used to measure increased loadings on Front End Processors, Statistical Multiplexors or LANs and LAN Bridges, as well as the impact on host applications and end-users.

The tools should provide:

* ease of use
* configurable message sizes
* scripting facilities
* flexible and graphical output facilities
* the capability to evaluate 'what if' scenarios.

7.3.2.6 Network costing tools

Network costing tools can provide a useful way of quickly and efficiently costing alternative network plans. They need to have:

* comprehensive lists of all product tariffs (BT, Mercury etc.)

* geographical references (eg post codes, telephone codes)

* regular updates and releases of product tariffs and geographical references

* interfaces to other tools, especially network planning and Cost Management.

7.3.2.7 Statistical analysis packages

These tools will be needed by all disciplines to analyse the output from other tools and monitors. A single package should be used within an organization, so that models and data can be easily exchanged. The tools should at least provide:

* ease of use

* good manipulative facilities

* graphical output facilities

* flexible reporting facilities

* interfaces to many of the other tools

* comprehensive import/export facilities.

7.3.2.8 Service Management tools

Tools to assist with the implementation of all of the Service Management disciplines will be required within the organization. Some of the tools will already exist within the existing Service Management discipline and others won't. Where they already exist, NSM will have to interwork with the existing function. Where either the tools or the discipline do not exist, then NSM will probably have to assume the functionality and cost justify both the function and the tools. Some existing Service Management tools have options dealing with networking aspects and others have no references to networks at all. Ideally products will provide assistance on all of the disciplines in a fully integrated and modular system. However at this point in time (1994) such products do not exist. There are products that cover individual disciplines and there are products that cover a number of the disciplines, but as yet no one product that covers all of them. These tools in general should provide:

* operation to IT Infrastructure Library guidelines and recommendations
* ease of use
* integration with other disciplines
* flexible and graphical reporting facilities
* modular design.

See the **IT Infrastructure Support Tools** volumes of the **ISE Appraisal and Evaluation Library** for more information on Service Management tools.

7.3.2.9 Risk analysis tools

For conducting risk analysis to CCTA Risk Analysis and Management Methodology (CRAMM) guidelines, a tool must be purchased. This type of tool may already be in use within the organization, if not then it should be cost justified. What is needed is:

* ability to cope with complex network dependencies
* ability to interface to existing configuration information
* ability to suggest protective measures appropriate to the assessed level of threat/vulnerability and the impact that a breach of confidentiality, integrity or availability is expected to cause
* evaluation of 'what if' scenarios
* ease of use.

7.3.2.10 Office automation products

Packages to assist with the automation and production of reports in a quick and cost effective manner will be required within all areas of NSM. The requirement is for a fully integrated set of electronic office products that provide full functionality. The main tools required are:

* word processors
* spreadsheets
* electronic mail

* statistical analysis
* desk top publishing.

7.3.2.11 Project management packages

There are numerous packages that exist for the control and management of projects, running on equipment from PCs to mainframes. Whenever project management tools are used for the control of a project they should be used within the PRINCE guidelines, to the organizational standards. The tools should provide as a minimum:

* resource, time and cost analysis facilities
* ability to view and display information in a variety of formats
* ease of use
* hierarchic project structure
* flexible reporting facilities.

7.3.2.12 Environmental monitors

There are several tools that exist for the monitoring of environmental conditions. Generally speaking they should be able to react to a particular event or threshold and indicate by means of a warning or alarm that action is needed, either on a local or a remote system. Indeed if the situation is critical enough the environmental monitor should be capable of initiating a tidy equipment shutdown. The facilities required are monitoring of:

* air conditioning units
* power supply, UPS or generator
* component or service availability
* fire detection/suppression systems
* gas and water detectors
* door, window and movement sensors
* essential units and services

together with interfaces to other systems:

* NMS, or Service Management tools
* automatic dial-out to pager or remote computer system.

7.3.2.13 Administration tools

Administration tools are required to hold the base information that documents the installed network systems and services in detail. In addition they must be capable of recording all the significant events that occur related to the network services for management, control and coordination purposes, for example:

* problem reports, diagnostics, repairs, resolution
* requests for change, authorization, tests, completion
* user details, account codes, service history
* support staff details, skill sets, current contacts
* configuration details live and fallback
* back-up and recovery dumps and procedures
* disaster recovery plans
* details of off-site securities and passwords
* scripted help information and instructions, eg how to reload routeing data on a specific types of system.

The generally accepted structure for this type of system is for it to be built within the Configuration Management Database (CMDB). Please refer to the **Configuration Management** module for more details. However it is essential that most of the above details are also stored off-site in hard copy documents, that will themselves need to be the subject of carefully implemented Change Management procedures.

7.3.3 NSM requirements for categories of tool

The following matrix shows the relationship between individual NSM disciplines and their requirements for the categories of tool described in section 7.3.2:

Tools	NSM	NSP	NSA	NSC	NSPC
Network Management Systems		Yes	Yes	Yes	
Network Services Software		Yes	Yes	Yes	
Network Testing Tools			Yes	Yes	
Network Planning Tools		Yes			Yes
Network Capacity Management		Yes	Yes	Yes	Yes
Network Costing	Yes	Yes	Yes		
Statistical Analysis Packages	Yes	Yes	Yes	Yes	Yes
Service Management	Yes	Yes	Yes		
Risk Analysis		Yes			
Office Automation	Yes	Yes	Yes	Yes	Yes
Project Management					Yes
Environmental Monitors			Yes	Yes	
Administration Packages	Yes	Yes	Yes	Yes	Yes

Figure 14: Tools usage matrix

7.4 Tool selection

All of the tools required by the NSM function should be procured, based on the recommendations contained within the organization's Network Plan and the following guidelines:

* the requirements and functionality of the tool should be formally defined

Section 7
Tools

* an evaluation method must be developed based on a requirements hierarchy, with the relative weight of each requirement being detailed

* once responses from suppliers have been received; three potential suppliers with known successful operational packages and reference sites, should be selected

* bidders' proposals should then be assessed based on a score for each weighted requirement. This assessment should include visits to reference sites, supplier demonstrations and a review of each bidder's documentation

* a package (or packages) should be selected for implementation. A formal project management tool based on a methodology such as PRINCE should be used for the implementation project if the effort involved warrants its use.

More general guidance can be found in the Information Systems Guides on Procurement (IS Guide B6) and Evaluation (IS Guide B7) and more specific (although not specific to Network Services Management) guidance can be obtained from the **Overview and Procedures** and **IT Infrastructure Support Tools** volumes in the **ISE Appraisal and Evaluation Library.**

7.5 Interface requirements

All of the tools used in the NSM function must be capable of:

* interfacing with all other tools in use within the NSM function

* interfacing with other service management tools, especially those of Configuration and Change Management, but also the Help Desk, Problem Management, Capacity Management and Availability Management

* meeting reporting, text processing and graphical presentation standards used in the organization.

7.6 Current tools

There are numerous tools currently available that will greatly assist with the development of an NSM function. However the problem with the majority of them is that they are proprietary by nature and are insular in their view of network components and disciplines. Tools currently available on the market do not cover the whole range of requirements mentioned in this module, although the situation is constantly improving. Tools should be selected on their conformance to international, open systems, networking and network management standards. A review of current tools and their capabilities is contained in annex E.

7.7 Advantages and pitfalls

Advantages

The advantages of using NSM tools are that they:

* automate the process of collecting and collating data from geographically dispersed equipment in a very efficient way

* provide more consistent, quicker results, using fewer resources

* are more accurate in repetitive tasks, and can handle large volumes of data

* allow more effort to be directed to the planning, control and management activities of NSM where the real benefits of NSM can be realized

* enable larger and more complex networks to be controlled in a more efficient and effective way.

The investment in the procurement and tailoring of tools, has to be balanced against the objectives of the NSM function and the benefit to the primary business of the organization.

Pitfalls

There are also many pitfalls in the use of tools for NSM, in that they:

* can often be proprietary in nature and design, locking the network and NSM to a particular supplier's strategy and products

* require many different methods of data collection and analysis, demanding of NSM the manipulation and control of numerous interfaces and data formats

* demand many skills to make full use of them

* are complex tools and often need configuring and tailoring to fit the requirements of the business

* may be used to compromise the security (ie confidentiality, integrity and availability) of network services

* are so numerous and diverse that the selection process can be very time consuming.

7.8 Summary

Most network services environments will have several types of NMS, one or more performance monitoring systems and a number of network support tools. In order to progress from this situation, the Network Services Manager should develop and maintain a strategy, based on the NSM 7 Layer model, which covers:

* the approach which should be taken towards NMS protocol standards (eg should network purchase be NMS protocol led?)

* the functional requirements of NSM in the organization

* a catalogue of tools in use or planned, and details of the functional requirements which the tools satisfy.

This will at least provide a route towards the goal of a fully integrated system, fulfilling all of the requirements of NSM in the organization.

The IT Infrastructure Library
Network Services Management

8. Bibliography

8.1 References

An Introduction to IT Infrastructure Planning. CCTA (due to be published 1994). ISBN 0-11-330617-2.

Computer Networks - Andrew S. Tanenbaum. Prentice-Hall 1981. ISBN 0-13-164699-0.

Discovering OMNI*Point* - A Common Approach to the Integrated Management of Networked Information Systems. Prentice Hall. ISBN 1-31-06121-6.

EPHOS Handbook. ISBN 92-826-3736-0.

GOSIP 4 Purchaser Set. I IMSO. ISBN 0-11-330568-0.

GOSIP 4 Supplier Set. HMSO. ISBN 0-11-330567-2.

GOSIP 4 Supplier Set Update. HMSO. ISBN 0-11-330608-3.

ISE Appraisal and Evaluation Library : Overview and Procedures. HMSO 1990. ISBN 0-11-330534-6.

ISE Appraisal and Evaluation Library : IT Infrastructure Support Tools. HMSO 1992. ISBN 0-11-330586-9.

Network Management - Dr. Kornel Terplan. Prentice-Hall 1987. ISBN 0-13-153065-8.

Network Management Problems, Standards and Strategies. Franz-Joachim Kauffels. Addison-Wesley 1992. ISBN 0-201-56534-X.

Statement of USER REQUIREMENTS for Management of Networked Information Systems. 1992. Network Management Forum.

UKSP 01 - Description of the Scheme. Head of the Certification Body, UK IT Security Evaluation & Certification Scheme, Room 2/0805, Fiddlers Green Lane, Cheltenham, Gloucestershire, GL52 5AJ.

Annex A. Glossary of terms

Acronyms and abbreviations used in this module

ACD	Automatic Call Distribution
ACSE	Association Control Service Element
ANSI	American National Standards Institute
ASE	Application Service Element
ASN.1	Abstract Syntax Notation 1
ATM	Asynchronous Transfer Mode
BABT	British Approvals Board for Telecommunications
BERT	Bit Error Rate Testing
BIS	Bring Into Service
BSI	British Standards Institution
CAB	Change Advisory Board
CAD	Computer Aided Design
CCITT	Comité Consultatif International Télégraphique et Téléphonique
CCTA	The Government Centre for Information Systems
CDB	Capacity Management Database
CEPT	Conference of European Posts & Telecommunications Administrations
CILE	Call Information Logging Equipment
CM	Configuration Management
CMDB	Configuration Management Database
CMIP	Common Management Information Protocol
CMIS	Common Management Information Service
CP	Contingency Planning
CPU	Central Processing Unit
CRAMM	CCTA Risk Analysis and Management Method
CSMA/CD	Carrier Sense Multiple Access/Collision Detection
DME	Distributed Management Environment

DTMF	Digital Tone Multi-Frequency
DSL	Definitive Software Library
ECC	Emergency Control Centre
ECMA	European Computer Manufacturers' Association
EDI	Electronic Data Interchange
EDIFACT	EDI for Administration, Commerce and Transport
EIA	Electronic Industries Association
E-Mail	Electronic Mail
EPHOS	European Procurement Handbook on Open Systems
ETSI	European Telecommunications Standards Institute
FEP	Front End Processor
FDDI	Fibre Distributed Data Interface
FM	Facilities Management
GOSIP	Government Open Systems Interconnection Profile
GOSIP MGT	GOSIP Management
GDN	Government Data Network
GTN	Government Telecommunications Network
IDA	Integrated Digital Access
IEE	Institution of Electrical Engineers
IEEE	Institute of Electrical & Electronics Engineers
IS	Information Systems
ISDN	Integrated Services Digital Network
ISE	Information Systems Engineering
ISEB	Information Systems Examination Board
ISO	International Organization for Standardization
IT	Information Technology
ITIL	IT Infrastructure Library
ITT	Invitation to Tender
ITU/TS	International Telecommunications Union/Telecommunications Sector
LAN	Local Area Network

Annex A
Glossary of terms

MAN	Metropolitan Area Network
MDNS	Managed Data Network Services
MHS	Message Handling System
MIB	Management Information Base
MLPT	Management of Local Processors and Terminals
MTBF	Mean Time Between Failures
MTTR	Mean Time To Recover
NACCB	National Accreditation Council for Certification Bodies
NCOP	Network Code of Practice
NDB	Network Database
NMF	Network Management Forum
NMS	Network Management System
NSA	Network Services Administration
NSC	Network Services Control
NSM	Network Services Management
NSP	Network Services Planning
NSPC	Network Services Project Control
ODETTE	The Organization for Data Exchange Through Tele-transmission in Europe
OFTEL	Office of Telecommunications
OMNI*Point*	Open Management Interoperability Point
OSF	Open Software Foundation
OSI	Open Systems Interconnection
PABX	Private Automated Branch Exchange
PBX	Private Branch Exchange
PC	Personal Computer
PER	Project Evaluation Review
PIR	Post-Implementation Review
PPG	Public Procurement Group
PRINCE	PRojects In Controlled Environments
PSE	Packet Switching Exchange

PSTN	Public Switched Telephone Network
PTT	Post, Telegraph and Telephone Administration
RAID	Redundant Array of Inexpensive Discs
RFC	Request For Change
RMON MIB	Remote Monitoring MIB
RSV	Reference Site Visit
SC&D	Software Control and Distribution
SIP	Service Improvement Programme
SLA	Service Level Agreement
SLM	Service Level Management
SMFA	Specific Management Functional Area
SNA	Systems Network Architecture
SNMP	Simple Network Management Protocol
SOR	Statement of Requirements
SQL	Structured Query Language
SSADM	Structured Systems Analysis and Design Method
SSR	Statement of Service Requirements
SSSO	Special Satellite Service Operation
TCP/IP	Transmission Control Protocol/Internet Protocol
TOR	Terms of Reference
TPDDI	Twisted Pair Distributed Data Interface
UPS	Uninterruptible Power Supply
VAN	Value Added Networks
VANS	Value Added Network Services
VPN	Virtual Private Network
VRU	Voice Response Unit
VSAT	Very Small Aperture Terminal
VTAM	Virtual Telecommunications Access Method
WAN	Wide Area Network

Annex A
Glossary of terms

Definitions

American National Standards Institute (ANSI)	Primary USA organization on OSI. It coordinates activities for standards implemented in the USA. The USA equivalent of BSI.
Automatic Best Path Routeing	The ability of a communications element to automatically choose the best transmission path based upon a pre-selected set of conditions ie traffic levels.
Asynchronous Transfer Mode (ATM)	A communications protocol which allows relatively high rates of transfer over conventional transfer media such as twisted pair. It uses a short, fixed length packet size which means that hardware switching may be used to increase transfer rates (over certain media). Speed ranges from 45Mbit/s to 155 Mbit/s (and is likely to increase in future).
Availability	In this module, availability is an umbrella term to also include serviceability, resilience, reliability and maintainability. A common definition of availability is given in the following paragraph.
	The ability of a component or IT service (under combined aspects of its reliability, maintainability and maintenance support) to perform its required function at a stated instant or over a stated period of time. It is usually expressed as the availability ratio, ie the proportion of time that the service is actually available for use by the customers within the agreed service time.
	For further explanation of availability, see the **Availability Management** module.
British Approvals Board for Telecommunications (BABT)	Non-profit making organization set up for the purpose of evaluation of subscribers' apparatus for connection to public telecommunications systems.
Backbone	A backbone is the major highway for information in complex network. It is not concerned with connecting terminal equipment to the network, rather with connecting local networks together. The term trunk is used in voice-only networks.
Bridge	A communications link between two homogeneous networks; or a link which uses a transport protocol that differs from those in the two networks, but uses a common high-level protocol. Simple bridges pass all traffic across each network. Intelligent bridges only pass appropriate traffic to the networks they link. Loops can be a problem when several bridges are used but most bridges detect loops.
Cable Management System	Provides a mechanism for planning, recording and controlling all changes to the cable infrastructure.

The IT Infrastructure Library
Network Services Management

Comité Consultatif International Télégraphique et Téléphonique (CCITT)	Now renamed International Telecommunications Union/ Telecommunications Sector (ITU/TS). A member of the ITU, a United Nations affiliate body. ITU/TS sponsors a number of standards dealing primarily with data communications networks, telephone switching, digital systems and terminals.
Conference of European Posts & Telecommunications Administrations (CEPT)	Involved with proposals for the standardization of equipment and network interfaces throughout Europe. Technical standardization has now been passed to ETSI.
Cost Model	Allocation of an initial cost during the planning stage, based upon typical industry valuations of each function and facility.
Carrier Sense Multiple Access/Collision Detection (CSMA/CD)	A common LAN protocol, made famous by Ethernet.
Disaster Recovery/Avoidance	The process of reacting to a disaster, or potential disaster, and managing the whole series of activities that allow a business to continue and finally return to a full operational state.
Dynamic Alternate Routeing	The ability of communications hardware to detect that a path has failed and automatically choose an alternative.
ECMA	A European body dedicated to the development of standards applicable to computer and communications technology.
Edge	A subset of the OSI standard network management interface as defined by the Network Management Forum.
EDIFACT	A United Nations initiative, started in 1985, to produce the definitive EDI standard.
EIA	A US national trade association which, although best known for its RS232-C specification, is currently working on Commercial Building Wiring specifications.
Ethernet	A LAN protocol based on CSMA/CD. Throughput up to 10Mbit/s, but realistically this is usually 4Mbit/s. Defined by ISO 8802/3 standard. Twisted Pair Ethernet is a cheaper alternative which uses hubs and star cabling.
European Telecommunications Standards Institute (ETSI)	Produces European Telecommunications Standards.

Annex A
Glossary of terms

Fibre Distributed Data Interface (FDDI)	A token passing network protocol designed for optical fibre links. Offers transfer speeds up to 100Mbits/s over long distances with high tolerance to interference. Also implemented over twisted pair, over shorter distances, with less tolerance to interference, as TPDDI.
Frame Relay	A communications protocol offering speeds of between 2 and 45Mbit/s. It uses a variable length packet (or 'frame') size which is particularly suitable for certain applications, but is not well suited to bulk data transfer.
Gateway	A device which converts the protocol of one or more networks to that of one or more others, but does not carry out a routeing function.
Host	A computer acting as a processing server node in a data communications network, enabling other nodes acting as client terminals to run applications on it and to obtain access to other resources.
Incident	An event which is not part of the normal operation of an IT service. It will have an impact on the service, although this may be slight and may even be transparent to users.
Institute of Electrical & Electronic Engineering(IEEE)	Involved for many years in standards activities throughout the world. The IEEE activity addresses local area networks and many other standards.
International Organization for Standardization (ISO)	The body which establishes international standards, including telecommunications standards. Its members comprise national standards bodies such as the British Standards Institution (BSI).
Local Area Network (LAN)	A telecommunications network which operates over relatively short geographic distances, typically within a room or a building.
Metropolitan Area Network (MAN)	A telecommunications network which implements the functionality of a LAN but over longer distances than a conventional LAN. Needs high speed lines, therefore relatively expensive. Used by organizations with several sites within one city (or metropolis), hence the name.
Managed Data Network Service (MDNS)	Provides services which 'manage' the data, eg protocol support and conversion, speed conversion, gateway services (eg for TELEX), technical management and administration; but falls short of providing 'applications' that would make it a Value Added Network.
Mean Time Between Failures (MTBF)	The average elapsed time from the time an IT service or component is fully restored until the next occurrence of a failure in the same service or component.

Mean Time To Repair (MTTR)	The average elapsed time from the occurrence of an incident to resolution of the incident.
Network Database (NDB)	Holds an inventory of all items of network equipment, where they are located, their performance criteria, costing information, application message sizes and transaction volumes, application performance requirements and a history log of performance statistics. May be subsumed by a Configuration Management Database (CMDB).
Network Server	A device connected to the network which provides a service to users of the network. For example, a print server, file server, mail server.
Network Services Administration (NSA)	Responsible for the tactical planning and implementation of network equipment and second line support for the NSC function.
Network Services Control (NSC)	Responsible for the day-to-day operation and control of the network and network services and provides the interface between the Help Desk and NSA.
Network Services Management (NSM)	The effective control and management of telecommunications (data and/or voice) network services.
Network Services Manager	Manager, appointed by the IT Services Manager, whose role is to run the Network Services Management function.
Network Services Planning (NSP)	Responsible for the strategic and tactical planning processes undertaken prior to implementing or enhancing a network service.
Network Services Project Control (NSPC)	Provides the project management and control of major new networks or network enhancement projects.
The Organization for Data Exchange Through Tele-transmission in Europe (ODETTE)	Represents and develops messages and EDI standards for the automobile industry.
Office of Telecommunications (OFTEL)	The apex of the UK National Telecommunications regulatory scheme, headed by the Director General of Telecommunications (DGT).
Open Management Interoperability Point (OMNI*Point*)	(Network Management Forum) - A set of standards, implementation specifications, testing methods and tools, which enable the development of interoperable management systems and applications.
Protocol conversion	The translation of the communications language (ie rules for conversation) of one network or communications link to that of another.

Annex A
Glossary of terms

Protocol stack	A layered set of protocols, each layer adding functionality to the layer underneath.
Post, Telegraph and Telephone Administration (PTT)	A (loose) term for the national authority which controls communication, often a branch of government. Often used as a shortened form of PTT Operator, meaning public telephone service provider such as BT or Mercury.
Router	A device linking two heterogeneous networks which routes traffic depending on its destination address. Effectively maintains two separate networks but creates a link between the two, so that only necessary traffic finds its way from one network to the other. Most routers support more than two protocols concurrently.
Sizing Exercise	Forecasting of future service levels, traffic volumes, usage patterns, performance requirements - inclusive of growth projections and contingency requirements.
Statistical Multiplexer	A multiplexer used to statistically control maximum amounts of data through a limited bandwidth channel.
Telecommunications network	A system which enables the transmission of information from a source to a destination.
Token Ring	A LAN protocol based on token passing. IBM Token Ring is the most common version, offering nominal speeds of 4 or 16 Mbit/s. Defined by ISO 8802/5 standard.
Trading Data Communications (TRADACOMS)	Trading Data Communications in the UK is the national standard developed by the Article Number Association. Used by 2000 companies throughout industry and commerce.
Value Added Network (VAN)	A network which offers users a 'value added' service in addition to data or voice transmission eg E-Mail, store and forward.
Virtual Private Network (VPN)	A network service which gives the functionality of a private network (such as abbreviated dialling, call forwarding, free local calls etc), but at lower cost because the physical network is shared.
Wide Area Network (WAN)	A telecommunications network which operates over large geographic distances. May consist of a number of interconnected LANs.
X.25	The ITU/TS standard for packet switched networks.
X.400	The ITU/TS standard for Message Handling Systems, such as electronic mail.
X.500	The ITU/TS standard for directories.

Annex B. Job descriptions and qualifications of Network Services staff

B.1 Network Services Manager

On setting up the function, the initial tasks are:

* to estimate the costs of the NSM function and secure approval for the design, implementation and operation of the network services systems and personnel and the NSM function

* to agree the scope and overall objectives of the NSM function with IT Management

* to conduct an awareness campaign bringing attention to the advantages and benefits of NSM and to publicize the NSM function throughout the organization

Ongoing major tasks are to:

* ensure that the Network Plan is produced and circulated to the appropriate IT and Business Management on a regular basis

* review and approve changes to the network planning, network design, network configuration, network management equipment and procedures, and ensure that all changes are subject to Change Management procedures

* assess the impact of Requests for Change on network services and attend the Change Advisory Board meetings when appropriate

* ensure that network services are adequately managed and administered and all relevant network management information is collected, recorded and reported upon

* supervise and monitor the performance of the NSM systems, personnel, procedures and hardware, including planning and scheduling, ensuring that adequate funding is available for the necessary tools

* maintain the quality of network services and instigate any remedial actions required, including

    - monitoring overall network service performance and taking action to correct deficiencies

The IT Infrastructure Library
Network Services Management

- monitoring and controlling the quality of individual network services
- monitoring, controlling and reviewing security and supporting procedures

* plan for the recruitment, training and development of NSM staff
* monitor and control the quality and cost of the network services to ensure that they are matched to business needs (within the IS strategy, Service Level Management (SLM) framework) and are within cost constraints
* manage network security, including generation and implementation of a Network Security Policy
* ensure that all appropriate regulations and standards are enforced
* ensure that regular audits and risk analysis exercises are conducted on the network and network services procedures
* manage relationships with suppliers of network hardware, software, systems and support services including contract negotiation, ensuring compliance to contractual commitments
* produce regular reports and attend regular network services reviews
* monitor the effectiveness and efficiency of the NSM function
* define the rules and responsibilities of the NSM function personnel
* define the interfaces and procedures for interactions between NSM and all other IT disciplines.

The Network Services Manager liaises closely with the IT Service Management managers, business managers, development teams, users (via Service Level Management, customer liaison and the Help Desk) and suppliers' representatives.

Annex B
Job descriptions and qualifications of Network Services staff

B.2 Network Services Planner

The major tasks are to:

* develop and maintain the Network Plan in conjunction with IS, IT and Business Plans and Strategies

* define and agree installation standards and policies for networks

* design the network for maximum resilience and availability, within cost constraints, in conjunction with the Availability Manager

* define and agree the requirements for new or modified network services and produce Statement of Requirements documents (SORs)

* produce alternative technologies and costings for new networks and network enhancements, for solutions that conform to the Network Plan

* produce Invitation to Tender (ITT) documents from network requirements

* review alternative network suppliers' proposals and recommend the most appropriate solutions

* select, recommend and cost justify network support tools

* provide an interface to IS, IT and business planners in the development of coherent corporate strategies

* assist the Capacity Management function in the planning of network capacity for new or modified network services

* assist the Availability Management function in the planning of network availability for new or modified network services

* assist the Contingency Planning function to plan for the recovery from any major network disaster and to plan for the required connectivity and capacity to all types of recovery facility eg hot, cold, mobile

* develop and maintain a catalogue of network services and agree a service recovery priorities in conjunction with Service Level Management

The IT Infrastructure Library
Network Services Management

* maintain an up-to-date knowledge of networking tools, techniques and technologies
* maintain an up-to-date knowledge of services and equipment from PTTs, facilities management companies and network equipment and service suppliers
* plan the environmental requirements for all new network equipment sites, including
  - physical access
  - intruder alarms
  - air conditioning
  - electrical supplies
  - water detection
  - fire detection and suppression
  - gas detection
  - false flooring
* monitor the running costs of the network and where possible make cost savings in collaboration with Cost Management
* plan improvements in network security in conjunction with the organization's IT and Network Security Policies
* establish and maintain procedures for Network Services Planning, Network Services Administration, Network Services Control and Network Services Planning & Control
* provide advice and guidance on all regulatory requirements relating to network equipment installation and operation
* to specify the level of spares to be maintained for all networking equipment.

A Network Services Planner liaises closely with the Network Services Administration, Network Services Project Controllers, Service Level Management, suppliers, systems analysts and programmers, applications analysts and programmers and IS, IT, and business planners.

Annex B
Job descriptions and qualifications of Network Services staff

B.3 Network Services Administrator

The major tasks are to:

* provide in-depth problem analysis and resolution, and act as third line technical support, for incidents escalated through the Problem Management function, from Network Services Control and Help Desk staff

* ensure that all network upgrades and changes are subject to Change Management procedures

* assist Configuration Management and ensure that the information contained within the Network Database and Configuration Management Database is consistent and correct for all network equipment at all network locations. This is essential to ensure that all elements of the network are subjected to Change Management procedures

* assist the Cost Management function by tracking period cost and charging information, and providing regular analysis and reports on network usage

* analyse all information on network performance and in conjunction with the Capacity Management function

    - produce network performance reports
    - tune the network for optimum performance
    - monitor network service levels
    - identify network bottlenecks and potential bottlenecks

* analyse network availability and produce regular and exception reports

* ensure that Software Control & Distribution (SC&D) procedures for release, build, test, distribution and implementation of all network software upgrades and installations are adhered to at all times, and that all network software is located in the Definitive Software Library

* maintain an independent network test facility for the testing of network software and hardware upgrades and corrections

* assist with the testing and implementation of all new network software releases

* develop and maintain the connections and mechanisms required by SC&D for non-network software
* evaluate new network equipment and technologies
* evaluate network management, support, analysis and diagnostic tools
* conduct site surveys at network sites and provide reports to Network Services Planning
* assist with disaster recovery events and tests
* provide a technical interface point with suppliers, systems designers and applications development groups
* establish and manage working procedures with all network supplier, support and PTT staff
* maintain normal and fallback equipment configuration information and media
* monitor the network for security violations and produce regular reports
* design and maintain Network Services Control procedures
* maintain a Technical Network Library containing all network documentation and procedures
  - all technical manuals on network equipment
  - networking documentation on standards, regulations and procedures
  - network schematics
  - building plans, cable routes, equipment locations, wiring closets and patching details
  - all disaster recovery plans
  - all network procedures
  - network support contracts, agreements, procedures and contact points
  - cable catalogue
  - software licencing agreements and proof of purchase documents
* maintain a complete duplicate copy of the Technical Network Library off-site.

Annex B
Job descriptions and qualifications of Network Services staff

A Network Services Administrator liaises closely with the Help Desk, Network Services Controllers, Network Services Planners, Problem, Capacity, Availability, Change and Service Level Management, and suppliers.

B.4 Network Services Controller

The major tasks are to:

* monitor network service operations, service levels and service quality on a day-to-day basis, taking corrective action where necessary

* interact closely with Help Desk and operations staff, acting as second line support, in the swift resolution of all network related service incidents

* record, classify and track network incidents detected by monitoring the network, in conjunction with the Help Desk

* maintain Help Desk question flow charts, system help screens, diagnostic scripts and checklists relating to network components of services, automating these procedures wherever possible

* assist in the determination and resolution of incidents that have been escalated to Problem Management, under the direction and control of Problem Management

* utilize network management systems for the operation and control of the networks and network equipment; interpret and act on all network management systems console messages, alarms and warnings

* operate all network equipment in accordance with laid-down network procedures

  - switch equipment on and off

  - dump and reload software and data from/to equipment

  - test equipment and links

  - activate and de-activate equipment

  - back-up and recovery of equipment configurations

- organize off-site security of back-ups and documentation
- switch to standby equipment/configurations

* maintain all data collection procedures and collect the following necessary information for the NSA reporting functions, automating them wherever possible

- response times
- equipment and network utilizations
- equipment and network performance
- network traffic profiles
- network and unit availability
- equipment reliability, serviceability, and maintainability
- network security

* liaise with network supplier and PTT support staff and engineers in the resolution of all network related incidents and in the organization of regular network hardware and software maintenance

* utilize and maintain network operational documentation and procedures, reporting amendments and updates back to NSA

* use network diagnostic equipment to diagnose network related incidents and problems

* maintain network toolkits and diagnostic equipment for the resolution of network incidents, and to ensure that all network spares are maintained at the specified levels

* use network management systems to pro-actively manage the organization's networks

* replace old or faulty equipment, under the direction of NSP, using Change Management procedures

* maintain a cable catalogue of all cable types, uses and configurations in use within the organization.

A Network Services Controller liaises closely with administrative staff, supplier representatives, Problem Manager, Change Manager, Change/Configuration Management staff, and Help Desk staff and other technical support staff.

Annex B
Job descriptions and qualifications of Network Services staff

B.5 Network Services Project Controller

The major tasks are to:

* develop and maintain standards for network implementation projects
* develop network implementation project plans for major new networks and network enhancements
* plan, coordinate and manage network projects, within budget and to timescale
* implement new networks and network enhancements with minimal impact on existing services and users
* conduct pilot studies and implementations
* perform test evaluations of new network systems
* ensure that all new software is contained within the Definitive Software Library
* ensure that all necessary configuration items are entered into the Configuration Management Database
* ensure that all systems are subjected to Change Management procedures
* ensure that the required operational procedures are developed, documented and passed to Network Services Administration for inclusion in the Technical Network Library
* identify and develop the appropriate training plans, handover procedures and sign-off procedures with NSM staff for all new network installations.

A Network Services Project Controller liaises closely with administrative staff, supplier representatives, Problem Manager, Change Manager, Change/Configuration Management staff, Help Desk staff and other technical support staff.

Annex C. Guidelines for reviewing current networks

Reviewing current networks and services is an important step in the planning process for a network services enhancement project. It can often be useful for greenfield site projects, if a similar installation to that being planned is available for a survey visit, (see also annex D - Guidelines for a reference site visit). The purpose of such a review is to establish a baseline from which estimates of changes needed to meet new requirements can be made.

When undertaking a review of current networks and services the main aspects that need to be established are:

Meeting user needs

* how suitable are the current networks and services for meeting the needs of the users?
* what do the users perceive as the main areas of strength and weakness?
* do the users perceive the networks and services to be reliable?
* to what extent are the current networks and services used?
* which functions or features are lacking on the current networks or services and how is this deficiency overcome currently?

Load, capacity, performance

* what is the distribution of workload by
  - network or service?
  - functions available on the network or service?
  - time of day, week or month?
* what level of performance is provided from the networks and services?
* is this level of performance acceptable?
* what is regarded as the main area of performance weakness?
* what is the current load factor profile as a percentage of the current capacity, and can this be matched to the performance experienced by users?

The IT Infrastructure Library
Network Services Management

Growth

* how easy is it to expand or contract/subdivide the networks or add new services or users?
* what level of growth (positive or negative) has been experienced?
* what is the match between predicted and actual growth for the last 12 months?
* what level of growth is currently predicted?

Costs

* what is the current cost profile for networks and services? (the distribution between fixed and variable usage costs should be noted)
* how does this match the predicted costs and the budget forecasts?
* are the networks and services more or less expensive to run than expected?
* what is the cost profile for growth?

Support and maintenance

* what level of in-house support is provided?
* do the necessary skills exist in-house?
* who provides this support?
* what is the overall cost of support?
* how much use is made of the support?
* what is the distribution of support calls? Consider this in terms of
    - incident calls
    - technical support enquiries
    - business function enquiries
    - requests for change
    - other
* what level of internal resource is required to support the networks or services in terms of time, skill levels, equipment?

Annex C
Guidelines for reviewing current networks

- * what form of external support is provided?
  - how much external support is required; and for what aspects?
  - what support response time is provided?
  - is the support response time satisfactory?
  - what levels of availability and reliability have been experienced?
  - what is the cost of external support?
  - how much control can be exercised on a day to day basis over external resources?

Security requirements

- * what security mechanisms, physical and logical, are currently in place?
- * what tests are applied to the security mechanisms?
- * how many security violations occur?
- * how severe are the security violations?
- * are there any alterations bringing new threats?
- * are the existing countermeasures working?
- * have changes in usage invalidated the results of impact analyses?

Annex D. Guidelines for a reference site visit

A reference site visit (RSV) is an excellent way of gaining insight and valuable information about a network that is being considered for use.

When undertaking an RSV it is important to be clear about what is to be achieved through the visit. Examples of objectives are an assessment of the:

* supplier in terms of meeting the costs, time-scales and functionality required for installation
* supplier or third party maintainer in terms of supporting the network
* growth characteristics of the network
* network's performance
* availability and reliability of the network
* strengths and weaknesses of the network management system
* adherence to standards
* availability of tools and their interoperability.

It is important to understand the differences between the network at the reference site and the one that is proposed for your organization. Take account not just of differences in model and version if there are any, but also differences in the use of the network. These questions should therefore be asked about the reference site network:

* is it the same model, release or version as the network and network management software being considered for your organization?
* what is the current and proposed use of the reference network?
* how do size and use of the reference network compare to the size and use of the network being considered for your organization?
* what is the level of current use (eg percentage load factor)?
* how long has the network been in use?
* what criteria were used to select the reference network?

The IT Infrastructure Library
Network Services Management

To obtain the maximum information from the RSV it is important to plan for the visit. A detailed questionnaire should be prepared which covers all aspects of the network that you wish to assess. As well as covering the points listed above, the questionnaire should also elicit the following information:

Network details

* installation date
* initial configuration
* who installed the network
* resources required
* number of users
* percentage load factor
* performance criteria
* connections to other systems.

Network operating system details

* installation date
* initial configuration
* integration with related operating systems
* level of automation of administration tasks (eg adding a new user).

Network management system details

* connections to other IT service management systems
* connections to operating systems (eg for automated software distribution and configuration audits).

Supplier details

* quality of project management
* quality of method and work
* quality of personnel
* level of liaison with organization's staff
* did the supplier meet the planned dates.

Implementation

* time required for installation
* quality of work
* were all aspects delivered as required
* quality of training.

Annex D
Guidelines for a reference site visit

Internal support
- who supports the system
- level and skill of staff required
- number of incidents handled
- number of underlying problems
- types of problems
- ease of modification
- ease of growth
- system management features
- diagnostics abilities.

Supplier support
- number of incidents and problems handled
- types of incidents and problems
- quality of response
- level of commitment
- expertise of support staff
- availability of system
- reliability of system
- spares levels and requirements.

Organizational issues
- reasons for selection of system
- main areas of use
- type and expertise of users.

Security requirements

Some organizations may not be prepared to supply answers to these questions, therefore sensitivity will be required:

- what security mechanisms, physical and logical, are available?
- what security mechanisms, physical and logical, have been implemented?
- what tests are applied to the security mechanisms and what are the results?
- how many security violations have occurred?
- how severe were the security violations?

Annex E. Network Services Management tools

This annex contains details of a selection of NSM tools that are currently (1994) available from a number of different suppliers. This is not a comprehensive review of all of the NSM tools that are available. However it does give some idea of the tools and the facilities that are available for each category of NSM tool. If specific tools are required by an organization it is strongly recommended that the tool selection process as contained in the **Overview and Procedures** and **IT Infrastructure Support Tools** volumes of the **ISE Appraisal and Evaluation Library** is followed.

Disclaimer: Whilst every attempt has been made to ensure that the information contained in the product summaries that follow is accurate, it is strongly recommended that the product details are checked with individual suppliers.

Tool categories

The tools used to provide the functionality of layer 3 of the NSM model fall into a number of different categories, and each may provide support for some or all of the requirements of the NSM supporting disciplines. The tools in this annex are reviewed in the same order and categories as in section 7.3.2.

Network management systems (NMSs)

Network management systems provide the day-to-day operation of a set of network components. There are three types of network management systems.

Data network management

Communications Management Series (Racal-Datacom): These CMS systems provide integrated LAN and WAN management on a variety of hardware platforms. The software is based on HP's Open View product.

DECmcc and **POLYCENTRE** (Digital Equipment Corporation): This is a family of products running on VMS and Ultrix platforms and can be used in conjunction with the POLYCENTRE portfolio to manage multi-vendor systems. They provide a graphical user interface with configuration control, alarm notification, fault management and performance statistics. Comprehensive reporting facilities are also provided. DEC however are moving away from the DECmcc and POLYCENTRE packages to concentrate on a product based on IBM's Netview 6000 system which will be called Polycentre Netview.

The IT Infrastructure Library
Network Services Management

Domain View (Cray Communications): Currently run a series of network management products each managing a separate domain. Cray are developing a new enterprise wide network management product, Domain View, based on the NMC Vision product from Network Managers, integrating their domain management products into one system.

ISOView and **Star-Tek** (3Com): The ISOView product runs on a PC and provides network management of 3Com's mid range network equipment. It provides a graphical user interface with configuration control, performance monitoring and statistics, and fault management. The Star-Tek network management system uses an SQL database on a PC and also provides alarm management, configuration control fault management, and comprehensive reporting facilities. Both systems use the SNMP protocol to monitor third party equipment.

Integrated Network Management System (ICL): The INMS system runs on a PC and can monitor and interact with any SNMP compliant systems. It provides a graphical user interface with scripting facilities to drive third party devices. It can also be integrated with ICL's OSMC products and provides fault management, cost control, configuration control, alarm handling, performance statistics and configurable reports.

LAN Network Manager (IBM): This is a PC based NMS providing control, fault management and performance statistics on IBM LANs. It can be integrated with an IBM Netview NMS to provide enterprise wide network management.

LattisNet Manager (Synoptics Communications): Runs on a PC and provides a graphical user interface down to the component and board level. It is based on HP's Open View and provides management of Ethernet and token ring systems. Automatic alarms can be generated and managed.

NetDirector (Ungerman-Bass): This is an enterprise wide network management system. It is based on a standard graphical interface and an SQL relational database. It uses the SNMP protocol to provide alarm handling and logging, fault management, and performance analysis. It has the ability to provide extensive network reports.

Netview and **Netview 6000** (IBM): These products provide management of IBM SNA networks. They can also be integrated with LAN Network Manager to provide management of IBM LANs. The Netview product runs on IBM mainframes and the Netview 6000 product is based on

Annex E
Network Services Management tools

HP's Open View system and can be used to provide management of non-SNA components using SNMP. They both provide graphical user interfaces for configuration control, fault management and performance management of large SNA networks and TCP/IP networks. They also provide interfaces to IBM's Infoman products.

Netware Management System (Novell): This is a set of products providing network management of a Novell network. It consists of a Netware Management Map (NMM) facility which provides the basic graphical user interface and automatically discovers the nodes on the network. Sitting above the NMM are a series of Services Managers (SMs). These consist of a Netware SM, a Hub SM, a LANtern SM, a Router SM and a Communications SM. Together they form a complete NMS with performance measurement and alarm handling facilities. Interfaces are also supported to IBM's Netview and HP's Open View.

NMC Vision (Network Managers (UK) Limited): Runs on either a PC Windows, SUN OS or AIX platform. It provides real time graphical network control and monitoring, multi-level alarm management, configuration control, network and device performance analysis, cost and resource analysis and fault management of a network. It supports the IP, IPX, TCP/IP, SNMP and X25 protocols and the OSF DME and NMF OMNI*Point* standards as well as a number of network supplier's proprietary interfaces and MIBs. It also provides a network developer's tool kit and is therefore used by a number of network equipment suppliers as a base for their own NMSs.

NMS/100 (Network Applied Technology (NAT)): This is a PC based system with a graphical user interface. It provides network management of an Ethernet network giving alarm handling, bridge management, traffic and performance measurement.

Open View (Hewlett-Packard): It provides real time graphical network control and monitoring, configuration control, multi-level alarm management, network and device performance analysis, cost and resource analysis and fault management of a network. It supports the CMIS/CMIP, TCP/IP and SNMP protocols and the OSF DME standard as well as a number of network suppliers' proprietary interfaces and MIBs. It also provides a network developer's tool kit and is therefore used by a number of network equipment suppliers as a base for their own NMS.

Optivity (Synoptics Communications): Is a network management system based on a UNIX system running SunNet Manager. It is designed to be an enterprise wide NMS and provides a graphical user interface down to component and board level. Optional modules can be added to provide fault management, policy management, trend management, router management and bridge management. It can also be seamlessly integrated with Novell NMS and can provide interfaces to DECmcc, HP's Open View and IBM's Netview 6000.

OverVIEW, OneVIEW and **TokenVIEW** (Proteon): TokenVIEW runs on a PC and provides network management of an IBM token ring network. It provides network monitoring and fault management facilities. The OverVIEW product also runs on a PC and provides a graphical user interface to LAN and WAN network management. A network database contains details of network configurations, alarms, and traffic and performance information. The OneVIEW product provides enterprise wide network management and is based on the NMC Vision product from Network Managers. It also provides graphical user interfaces to the component and board level.

SPECTRUM and **Remote LANVIEW** (Cabletron): A full graphical user interface is provided from this NMS which is based on HP's Open View. It provides control, fault alarm and performance management of all of Cabletron's LAN equipment. It runs on a PC and provides interfaces to IBM's and Novell's NMSs. The SPECTRUM system runs under Unix and is based on an object-oriented database. It gives enterprise wide network management and provides a graphical user interface with network monitoring and control, alarm handling, configuration control and performance analysis. It also provides interfaces to IBM's Netview.

SpiderManager (Spider Systems): This runs on a PC and supports Spider products and third party products using the SNMP protocol. It is a Microsoft Windows based system providing a graphical user interface with event logging, alarm handling, configuration control and performance facilities.

Timeview (Ascom Timeplex): Timeview is a network management system using primarily SNMP but moving towards SNMP 2 and is based on HP's Open View.

Annex E
Network Services Management tools

Voice network management	**Cubix** (Cubix Limited): Interfaces to a PC and provides comprehensive traffic analysis and call management facilities. It also supports costing and charging facilities.
	Datapulse (Datapulse Limited): Runs on a PC and provides detailed traffic analysis and reports over multi-site networks. It can be combined and integrated with costing and accounting software and an electronic directory and message storage facility.
	Genesis (Telecommunications Information Systems Limited): Runs on a PC network and provides call management facilities. It also provides an online directory system and online display of traffic summaries.
	Isocom (Business Telecommunications Services Limited): Runs on a PC and consists of a suite of systems providing asset management, network management, network modelling, network costing and traffic and call management facilities over multi-site networks. Together they provide a complete telecommunications management system with flexible automatic reporting, alarm systems, online display facilities and an electronic directory.
	Network Perception (Christie Telecom Limited): Runs on a PC and provides real-time graphical network control and monitoring, fault management, alarm management, user scripting using the CAER command language and cost and resource analysis. It supports interfaces to a number of sites and PBXs, and also supports interfaces to most PC spreadsheet packages.
	Objective Reality Series (Objective Science Group): Is a set of modules providing comprehensive call management facilities with real-time graphical displays, an alarm system, extensive reporting facilities, automatic personal messaging system, pro-active fault detection, logging and a reporting system.
Cable management	**CADVANCE** (ISICAD (UK) Limited): This is a cable management system providing integrated PC Windows, CAD and relational database facilities via multiple levels of access. Cadvance runs under Microsoft Windows and allows multiple drawing and views to be displayed simultaneously. Running under Windows means that it is easy to combine with other databases and spreadsheets. It also supports the import and export of CAD drawings and can create and present 3D images.
	Caplum (Datel Communications Systems): Runs on a PC and provides an integrated cable management system with an underlying relational database. Multi-level access

facilities are provided with circuit routeing and tracing facilities, covering, data, voice, LAN and WAN network operation over multiple sites. It supports an interface to PABXs with automatic database updating facilities. Automatic and user configurable reporting facilities are also provided.

Crimp+ (Datel Communications Systems): This is similar to Caplum and runs on a PC providing multi-level access facilities to an integrated CAD and relational database. It provides cable routeing and tracing facilities for voice, data LAN and WAN networks over multiple sites with automatic database updating from PABX systems. Automatic and user configurable reporting facilities are also provided with the ability to import CAD building plans. Sorting facilities are also provided for the generation of telephone directories and other associated documentation.

TRAIL (ITT Datacom): This is a cable management system that can run on several hardware platforms and supports cabling schematics, multi-user operation and multi-site operation. It also provides cable routeing facilities and configurable reporting facilities.

Network services software

The principal function of network services software is to provide monitoring and reporting information about the performance of a service, or set of services. These are specific to the host systems that are responsible for providing the network service. The facilities may be provided by the operating system itself, the communications software, TP software or the applications themselves. The products themselves are too numerous to mention in their entirety so a couple of examples have been given.

Service monitoring systems

MVS, Netview and **CICS** (IBM): These systems provide numerous facilities for monitoring service availability and response time figures especially using Response Time Monitor (RTM).

VME and **TPMS** (ICL): These systems also provide numerous facilities for monitoring service availability and response times.

Annex E
Network Services Management tools

Network testing tools

Network testing equipment systems are far too numerous for them all to be mentioned; however, a few examples of each type have been included to give an idea of the sort of facility that can be provided.

Break-out boxes/ interface testers

This type of equipment can be provided by most network equipment suppliers:

Interfaker Range (Interfaker): This is an extensive set of diagnostic tools ranging from a simple interface break-out box to sophisticated diagnostic systems containing advanced break-out boxes, analogue line modules, digital multi-meters and logic probes.

Black Box: Provide a comprehensive range of break-out boxes for use with Centronics, V.24, V.35 and X.21 interfaces.

Circuit and cable testers

Connections (UK) PLC: Provide a comprehensive range of cable test equipment ranging from simple stand-alone cable testers through intelligent testers, to scopes attached to PCs. These systems vary in both price and complexity considerably, from testers that simply display cable connections using LEDs to those with PC screen display that compare cables to libraries of cable definitions.

SLT3 (MOD-TAP): Master and remote cable testers with LEDs to indicate shorts, open circuits and reversals. Test sets are available for STP, UTP and fibre optic systems.

Wandel & Goltermann and **HP**: Both of these suppliers can provide a complete range of test sets for testing the quality of analogue, digital and ISDN circuits. Some sets are multiple test sets and some are single purpose sets, it is a question of matching the set to the requirements.

Media scanners

HP 340, J2201A and **J2196A** (HP): These are hand held LAN media scanners for isolating wiring problems on LANs.

MT 310/340/350 (Microtest Inc): These are a set of hand held scanners utilizing cable tracers and time domain reflectometers (TDRs) in order to identify wiring problems.

FLUKE 650: (FLUKE) This is a hand held cable scanner for the testing a variety of different cable types.

LAN-MD (Cabletron): This is an Ethernet media scanner and is also capable of testing Ethernet transceiver functionality.

Network monitors/ analysers and remote probes

Ethmon2, EthviewPro 2, TokMon and **TokView** (Kenson Network Engineering Limited): These are a series of LAN protocol analysers and monitors, providing comprehensive fault finding and performance analysis facilities on both Ethernet and token ring LANs. They can also be used for traffic generation and programmable messaging.

HP 4957A/PC and **4959A** (HP): These are WAN protocol analysers and can be use in conjunction with frame relay, ISDN, X25 and SNA protocols. They have in-built Bit Error Rate Testers (BERT) and can be used to pin point problems, test and monitor line quality and produce performance statistics.

HP 4972A (HP): This is an Ethernet LAN protocol analyser that can be used for network fault finding, performance analysis, protocol decoding, traffic generation and programmable messaging. Used regularly it can be used to develop trends and network statistics.

HP Network Advisor (HP): This a comprehensive network LAN protocol analyser. It is a multi-tasking system and has protocol decoders for all of the commonly used LAN protocol stacks. It is a PC based system with in-built protocol fault finding advice and guidance. It also has traffic generation, node statistics, error statistics and performance analysis capabilities.

HP LAN Probes (HP): HP provide a range of LAN probes that can be used to monitor and control the performance of LAN systems. Some of these probes are proprietary and some support the TCP/IP(SNMP) RMON MIB standard.

LANtern[tm] (Novell): This is a Novell supplied SNMP Ethernet probe that can be used in conjunction with Novell's LANtern Services Manager.

LANB/150[tm] (Network Applied Technology): This is a LAN probe providing performance and traffic statistics on an Ethernet LAN segment.

LANVIEW[tm] and **MACLANVIEW**[tm] (Cabletron): These are LAN protocol analysers that can be used for network fault finding, performance analysis and protocol decoding, . They can be run on either an IBM PC compatible or an Apple Mac II respectively and used regularly can be used to develop trends and network statistics.

Spider Probe B235 (Spider Systems): This an Ethernet LAN probe providing statistics gathering and alarm generation. It supports the SNMP RMON MIB standard for remote network monitoring.

Annex E
Network Services Management tools

Network planning/design tools

L.NET (CACI): This is a local area network planning and performance prediction tool that runs on an IBM PC compatible or workstation. It can be used to predict the performance of both Ethernet and token ring networks and can be used to evaluate alternative solutions or predict bottlenecks. It can produce extensive graphs and reports on network traffic.

COMNET III (CACI): This is a combined LAN, MAN and WAN network capacity planning and performance prediction system. It can be used with X25, ISDN, ATM, FDDI and TCP/IP WANs as well as CSMA/CD and Token passing LANs. It also has comprehensive graphical and tabular report facilities.

Network Capacity Management tools

Network Database (NDB) — The NDB should form part of the overall IT Capacity Management Database (CDB). If neither a Capacity Management function nor CDB exist, then it may be necessary for NSM to create a CDB to contain the NDB. A database package should be selected that provides comprehensive reporting facilities, and preferably one that can be connected to NMSs for automatic updating. Additional information can be found in the **Capacity Management** module.

Network performance monitoring — LAN probes and analysers can be used as network performance analysers on LANs. Left connected to LANs or connected on a regular basis they can be used as invaluable performance monitors. Most of the probes and analysers above can be used for this function.

WAN performance monitoring is normally provided by the network equipment manufacturer's NMS. These are mainly proprietary but some of the open NMSs, such as OpenView and NMC Vision can also be used to collect WAN performance data.

Network modelling — Network modelling packages can be bought for in-house operation, to monitor the organization's own network. Some of these packages are listed below. An alternative is to use the consultancy service provided by an external systems house such as Pactel, CACI or Durham University.

Trend analysis — **SAS** (SAS Institute): This is a statistical analysis package that also provides extensive trend analysis facilities.

Analytical modelling	**NETWORK II.5** (CACI): This is a computer or communications network analysis package that can run on a mainframe, workstation or IBM PC. Elements can be selected from a library of definitions or can be user specified. These can then be configured into a network which can be fed through the verification process. Once verified, simulations of the telecommunications network can be performed to evaluate alternative technologies and solutions and produce reports on utilizations, conflicts and contentions. Extensive tabular and graphical report facilities are available as well as block diagrams of the network.
Network costing tools	The majority of system management tools, for voice, data and cable management provide integral costing and accounting facilities.
Statistical analysis packages	**SAS** (SAS Institute): This is probably the most commonly used and most comprehensive statistical analysis package. It is available on both IBM PCs and mainframes and provides all of the statistical and reporting facilities that are likely to be needed.
Service Management tools	Comprehensive details of Service Management products can be found in the individual IT Infrastructure Library modules. Four examples have been provided to show the type of products that are available.
	Infoman (IBM): This used in conjunction with Resource Object Data Manager, gives an object-oriented database that provides Configuration Management, Change Management, Help Desk and Problem Management functionality. Infoman can also be interfaced to IBM's Netview products.
	Layer 8 (Lynx Communications Limited): This is a system that supports the OMNI*Point* interface and can provide asset management, Change Management, Help Desk and Problem Management facilities. It is based on an Oracle database and can also provide costing and charging facilities.
	Open Systems Management Centre (OSMC) (ICL): This system is based on an Ingres database. It provides modules to perform Help Desk, Problem Management, Change Management, Software Control and Distribution and Capacity Management functions. This can be integrated with ICLs INMS products.
	Red Box (Ultracomp Limited): This is a system based on an Oracle database and is designed to implement the functional requirements of Service Management identified in CCTA's IT Infrastructure Library. It is a Unix based

Annex E
Network Services Management tools

system and provides Configuration Management, Change Management, Help Desk and Problem Management functionality.

Risk analysis tools **CRAMM** (CCTA): CRAMM is a methodology available as a software support tool (from several private sector suppliers) that formalizes the process of security and risk assessment.

Office automation products These products are required to produce and distribute reports effectively and efficiently around an organization. Normally an organization will have a standard set of products that should be used throughout the organization. These are often based on a set of PC products, the type of products that can be used are as follows:

* Word Processing Systems
  - Ami Pro from Lotus
  - Word from Microsoft
  - WordPerfect
  - Wordstar
* Spreadsheet Systems
  - Excel from Microsoft
  - Lotus 1-2-3 from Lotus
  - Quattro Pro from Borland
  - SuperCalc from CA
* Mail Systems
  - cc:Mail from Lotus
  - Microsoft Office
  - WordPerfect Office
* Desk Top Publishing Systems
  - Adobe
  - PageMaker from Aldus
  - TimeWorks.

**Project management
packages**

These packages are often based on PC products, the types of product that can be used are as follows:

* CA-SuperProject
* Microplanner
* Microsoft Project
* Project Manager's Workbench (PMW).

**Environmental
monitors**

These systems are quite often based on hardware control panels that either give local alarms or in some cases can be connected to modems to give remote alarms. More comprehensive programmable software solutions can also be provided.

Vigilant (Ultracomp Limited): This is a comprehensive programmable local and remote event/alarm system for temperature, humidity, water, intruder, electricity supply, mainframe and network environments.

Administration tools

Administration tools should be provided as part of the overall Configuration Management database. More information can be found in the appropriate IT Infrastructure Library module.

Annex F. Network management standards - future directions

F.1 Introduction

This section describes network management standards and highlights their advantages and disadvantages.

The task of managing a large, distributed network is immense. By their very nature, networks are complex. When viewed from an engineering perspective there is a large number of components involved in a network, ranging from passive components to very intelligent processing systems. Networks in general are growing in both size and complexity. If corresponding improvements are not made in the tools and techniques that are used to manage and control them, then they will demand ever increasing levels of resource to operate.

The standards making process strives to find a simple but effective approach to managing this spread of technology - based on existing standards where possible and deriving new standards where required.

There is much effort contributed to make new standards similar to existing techniques and products, or at the very least, make some accommodation for them. This can lead to a less than optimal solution, or at least add significant delay in the standards making process.

F.2 Network management systems

The major network management systems that exist at the moment can be classified in terms of the network management standards that they support.

Proprietary systems
: These systems support proprietary protocols and equipment and are normally therefore tied to the equipment of one network supplier.

TCP/IP (SNMP) systems
: SNMP systems support the de-facto network management standard protocol. This is probably the most commonly used protocol for network management systems.

OSI CMIP/CMIS systems
: This is probably the most comprehensive and most complicated set of network management protocols. It is a set that is still being developed, but has the backing of ISO.

OMNI*Point* systems
: This is a recent entry into the network management protocol arena. The OMNI*Point* programme is the product of the Network Management Forum and has entered the scene because of the delay in the development of the OSI network management protocols.

The IT Infrastructure Library
Network Services Management

GOSIP MGT systems	These systems implement the UK GOSIP recommendations on network management protocols. This is a stable specification and advises that CMIP/CMIS protocols should be used and so GOSIP MGT Systems are therefore a variant of OSI systems.
Hybrid systems	These systems support a combination of the above list of network management protocols.

The predominant push in the area of networking standards is on the basis of using the CMIP/CMIS standards for managing networks and network services. This approach is significantly influenced by object-oriented technology concepts. While this will lead to standards that are theoretically sound, there is some concern that the processing and transport requirements needed to support this technology will be excessive and only be suitable for large scale network systems with sophisticated components. Indeed because of the growing sizes of processing and memory required to implement the standard, it is unlikely that some of the more basic components will ever implement the protocol. In addition, the degree of detail that needs to be addressed with this approach indicates that significant time and effort will be required to develop standards that will address even the most basic management activities in the network. The issues required to develop higher level standards will not be considered for some considerable time.

To complicate the situation still further, a number of the major suppliers have indicated that they will reserve the right to augment any standards produced with proprietary extensions, with the intention of differentiating their products with respect to others. However, it is not clear how this will significantly help the Network Services Manager, but for all of the problems associated with the OSI CMIP/CMIS protocols, they are still seen as the strategic long term future for the network management process.

F.3 Network management standards

The current structure and future developments of each of the network management standards are examined in the following sections.

F.3.1 TCP/IP (SNMP)

The TCP/IP family of protocols are controlled by the Internet community and the Internet Advisory Board (IAB). The community plan to migrate to OSI standards, but will not do so until the OSI network management standards

Annex F
Network management standards – future directions

become more stable. SNMP has become the de-facto industry standard for LAN network management and is probably the most widely used network management protocol.

The structure of SNMP
There are three components to the Simple Network Management Protocol (SNMP) standard: the Structure of Management Information (SMI), the Management Information Base (MIB), and the protocol itself, SNMP.

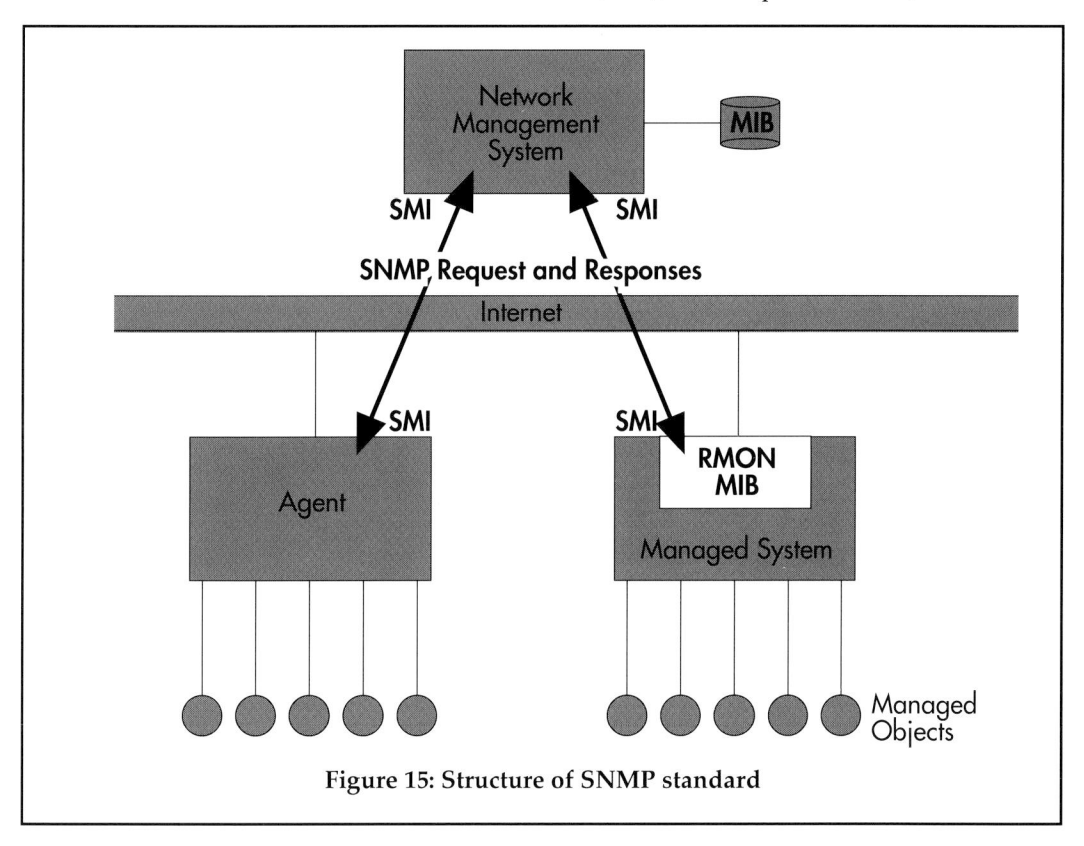

Figure 15: Structure of SNMP standard

SMI
SMI is a set of rules that defines the characteristics of network objects and how management protocols extract information from them. SMI is expressed in a subset of the international standard language Abstract Syntax Notation 1 (ASN.1).

MIB
The MIB is a collection of objects that represent the devices in the network and their internal components, based on a hierarchic structure. The MIB knows all managed objects and their attributes and is a database, possibly distributed throughout the network. A problem with the MIB concept is that the majority of network suppliers, because of the limitations of the MIB standard, have developed their own

extensions to the MIB, thereby forming proprietary MIBs. This situation is further complicated by the fact that there are two MIB standards MIB I and MIB II.

Even more recent extensions to the MIB concept have allowed the development of Remote Monitoring MIBs or RMON MIBs. This allows a remote managed system to provide information on a number of managed objects. Many network suppliers are now providing purpose built hardware that does nothing else but provide RMON MIB functionality, purely for the purposes of network management. These are invaluable tools for monitoring remote equipment.

SNMP

SNMP is the protocol itself and is the mechanism for transferring information between the management station and the managed agents, devices and managed systems. it is usually implemented using the User Datagram Protocol (UDP) and Internet Protocol (IP) of the TCP/IP suite of protocols.

Advantages

SNMP has several advantages:

* it is the most commonly used system for network management

* most network equipment supports SNMP

* it places relatively small demands on system resources.

Disadvantages

The disadvantages are:

* it is insecure and therefore it is only safe for monitoring the network, not actively managing it (re-configuration is not restricted to specific users)

* it uses polling and therefore is more suitable for small domains rather than large networks, because of the traffic that polling generates

* it is a comparatively restrictive interface.

The future of SNMP

SNMP will be superseded by a revised version, SNMPv2. It is an extension of the existing SNMPv1 and is designed to improve network efficiency and increase network security by providing the following enhancements:

* more efficient retrieval of bulk data

* greater number of detectable errors

* improved re-structured interface for handling MIBs

* a reformatted trap message

Annex F
Network management standards – future directions

* a new MIB for manager to manager communications
* a selective configuration of MIB facilities to managers
* allows SNMP to run over Appletalk, IPX and OSI protocol stacks.

SNMPv2 is not backwards compatible with SNMP, so users who have implemented SNMP face a migration task to SNMPv2.

The long term future of SNMP is seen as a migration of SNMP to OSI protocols. This will probably happen as a series of steps:

* Step 1 - Initially management systems running SNMP over UDP within the TCP/IP protocol stack
* Step 2 - Management systems moving to an interim phase of running Common Management over TCP/IP (CMOT). This would involve running CMIS facilities over a TCP/IP transport service
* Step 3 - As the standards mature there will be a gradual migration to full CMIS/CMIP operation.

OMNI*Point* has produced a guide on SNMP/CMIP migration and co-existence and CCTA produce a guide on TCP/IP migration to OSI.

F.3.2 OSI CMIP/CMIS (GOSIP MGT)

The OSI network management standards are covered in a series of ITU/TS (CCITT) and ISO documents which are at various levels of ratification. OSI also has the concept of the Management Information Base (MIB) being the network component database, possibly distributed through the network at the various layers of the OSI 7-Layer model.

The structure of OSI CMIS/CMIP

The CMIS/CMIP network management operation requires the operation of a full OSI protocol stack in order to function, as shown in figure 16 overleaf.

The coordination of activity between two OSI systems is provided by the Association Control Service Element (ACSE). This makes the association between a client Application Service Element (ASE) and a server ASE using the underlying OSI protocol stack. Once this link has been established then the two systems can exchange information using the CMIP protocol. CMIS is a system management ASE which uses a set of service primitives for the exchange of a standard set of commands and responses, for the transmission of data between the two systems.

The IT Infrastructure Library
Network Services Management

Figure 16: Structure of OSI Management

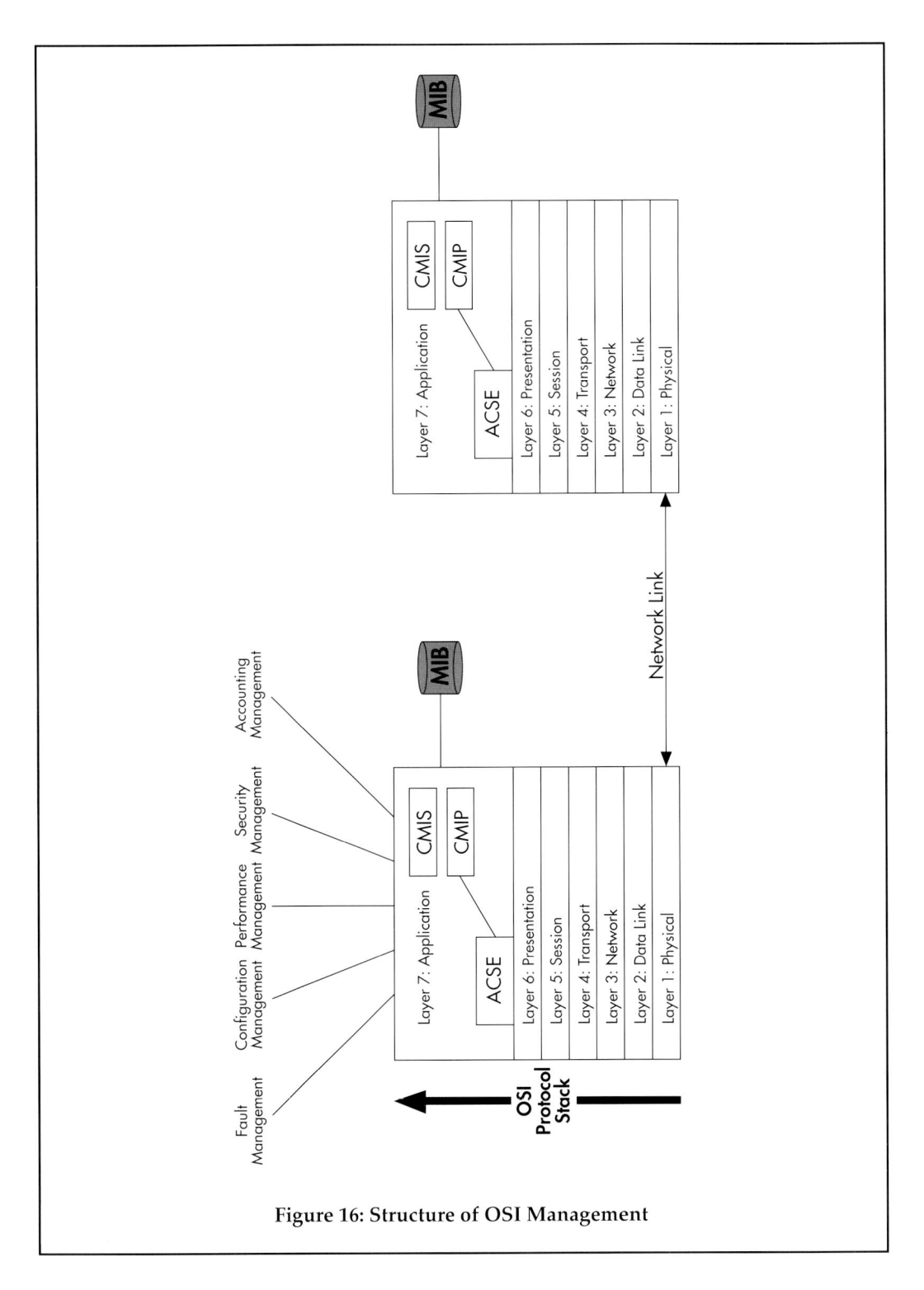

Annex F
Network management standards – future directions

The OSI management framework also defines five categories of function called Specific Management Functional Areas (SMFAs):

* Configuration SMFA - provides the identification, monitoring and control of managed objects

* Error SMFA - processes error states

* Performance SMFA - evaluates object behaviour and conversations

* Security SMFA - controls and distributes information, whilst protecting the integrity of the data, and highlights any security alerts

* Accounting SMFA - calculates the costs associated with using managed objects.

These SMFAs are responsible for monitoring and controlling the following aspects of a managed object:

* the existence of the object

* the object's attributes

* the object's states

* the relationship between the object and other objects.

Advantages

There are advantages in using the OSI CMIP/CMIS protocols for network management:

* allows full functionality between the managing and managed systems

* allows flexibility between the managing and managed systems

* is capable of supporting large networks

* it is the ISO standard and therefore seen as the way forward.

Disadvantages

The disadvantages are as follows:

* it is a very recent standard and is not fully defined

* it will take time to establish itself

* it is supported by a small range of network equipment

* it can require a full OSI stack and is expensive in terms of resources (developments such as CMOL (CMIP over LLC) provide solutions to the full stack problem, allowing LAN devices to be managed via a cutdown stack)

The IT Infrastructure Library
Network Services Management

* it concentrates on the operational aspects of the network.

The future of OSI CMIS/CMIP

The OSI CMIS/CMIP standards are seen as the long term strategic objective for network management systems

F.3.3 OMNI*Point* (NMF)

OMNI*Point* is a set of standards introduced by the Network Management Forum (NMF), which is a group formed by a number of major users, network operators and network suppliers. Its aim is to produce working standards for the integration and inter-working of network management and systems management systems. OMNI*Point* provides specifications of the interfaces for the implementation of the open management of networked systems. It does not define the actual management applications themselves.

The structure of OMNI*Point*

OMNI*Point* 1 consist of a set of OMNI*Point* interfaces that can be integrated into a management system. The management systems use the OMNI*Point* interface or 'Open Management Edge' (Edge) via a standard Applications Programming Interface (API). This X/Open Management Protocol API (XMP) specification, provides a management service interface to support the use of both CMIP and SNMP. The CMIS specification is then used for the exchange of management information between cooperating management systems.

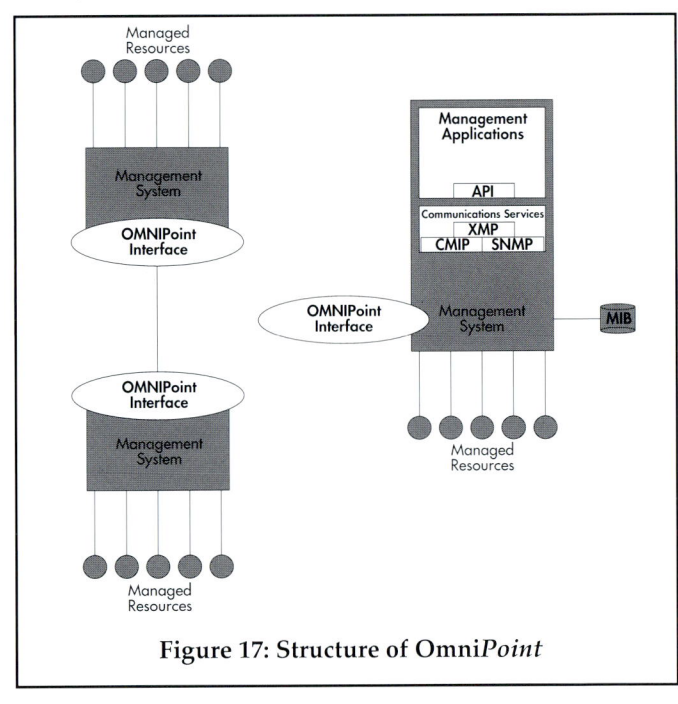

Figure 17: Structure of Omni*Point*

Annex F
Network management standards – future directions

Advantages	There are advantages in using OMNI*Point* standards for network management:

* supports any functionality between management systems and NMSs
* is capable of supporting large networks
* data is only entered once, and is then transferred through the network
* data is consistent across management systems
* it is based on OSI standards but supports other protocols
* it is an ideal migration tool between management systems and protocols
* it is supported by users, network operators and network suppliers.

Disadvantages	The disadvantages are as follows:

* it is a very recent standard and is not fully evolved and defined
* it will take time to establish itself
* it is supported by a small range of network systems.

The future of OMNI*Point*	The NMF have only announced details of the contents of OMNI*Point* 1, the first stage of the planned series of OMNI*Points*.

F.3.4 SNA (IBM)

The structure of SNA	IBM network management revolves around the use of Netview. Until recently Netview was only available on large IBM mainframes, but there are now Netview products available to run on mini and PC systems.
Advantages	There are advantages in using the SNA protocol for network management:

* it is well defined
* it has a large installed base
* it can be integrated with other management systems.

Disadvantages	The disadvantages are as follows:

* it is a proprietary protocol and architecture
* few network suppliers support the SNA network management interfaces.

The future of SNA	IBM have announced their commitment to OSI standards.

F.3.5 Summary

In summary, network management standards are developing fast and with the push from the NMF, faster than they otherwise would have done. It will probably be years before the full benefits of truly integrated network management and systems management are achieved. However, with careful selection of tools and protocols, significant benefits can be achieved.

Annex G. Planning and implementing network services

G.1 Introduction

This annex describes the *planning and implementation of new or enhanced network services* rather than the planning and implementation of the management function as described in the body of this module.

The planning and implementation of new or enhanced network services should be carried out as a formal project, using PRINCE.

The Terms of Reference (TOR) for the project must clearly highlight the business issues involved and include a statement of objectives. In addition, the TOR must outline:

* the breadth and depth of consultation expected with existing IT functions such as Applications Development, Capacity Management

* the intended use of the network services

* the service levels required

* the cost profiles sought, and cost constraints

* the criteria that will be applied to determine the viability of any proposed solutions

* how the network systems and services are to be supported and managed after the implementation is complete and whether the provision of this support and management forms part of the project (this is usually the case).

G.2 Appoint team

The initial step in the project is to appoint a team to carry out the planning and implementation of the new services. When selecting individuals for the team, it is important to ensure that:

* the correct breadth and depth of both business and technical skills are included

* staff from business planning, technical IT planning and IT Services Management are included in the team

* those selected do not have conflicting workloads or responsibilities.

Computer Operations, Service Level Management, the Help Desk, Configuration Management, Cost Management, Capacity and Availability Management, Contingency Planning and Security Management staff must all be kept informed during the planning process and should be considered for involvement in the project team. Input from these functions is an essential component of the planning process and involvement at this stage will reap improved assistance and cooperation later on.

Having appointed the team, five steps are involved at this point in the planning process. These are to:

* establish what precisely is required by end users, ie carry out a user requirements analysis. This must conform to the IS strategy and the overall aim of the business as stated in the TOR for the project

* carry out a gap analysis - analyse the existing systems and services and identify the shortfalls in meeting the proposed user and business requirements

* conduct an outline sizing exercise

* prepare a formal statement of requirements (SOR)

* carry out an initial costing exercise.

G.3 Requirements analysis

Unless the project forms part of a larger infrastructure project (see **An Introduction to IT Infrastructure Planning**), for which user requirements have already been analysed and documented, it will be necessary to carry out a detailed analysis of user requirements. The analysis can be achieved by using well established techniques such as:

* interviews with representative users and managers

* written questionnaires

* user groups and surveys.

The analysis must cover not only functions, but also the service levels and the support required.

In the analysis, it is important to separate out the business requirements (need) from the preferred and wish-list type of request (desired). It must identify what users currently find unsatisfactory and why. All the requirements must be documented, but it is important that their priorities and weighting are clearly defined by business managers.

G.4 Gap analysis

Once the analysis of user requirements is complete, compare the results with existing systems and services. The comparison will indicate whether the project requirements are completely new or an enhancement of existing facilities. The latter is more likely, unless some new business function, change of working practice or exploitation of new technology is being considered.

Reference site

If the analysis indicates that the requirements are new then investigate a similar type of installation elsewhere. This enables the project team to validate the requirements (and assumptions) on which the current project plan is based. See annex D for guidance on carrying out a reference site visit.

G.5 Conduct outline sizing exercise

Identify the job or task types to be supported by the planned network services. This will enable required usage patterns, performance and availability requirements to be predicted on a per-job or task basis.

By accumulating these data, the planning team can forecast the service levels and traffic volumes required. A knowledge of:

* the number of existing and planned sites
* the organizational mix at each site
* the number of people per job function

is required for these forecasts.

In the case of a completely new implementation, the only source of information may be outline plans. In all cases, the information collected must cover the planned period that the project is to address.

Analyse current usage

For existing networks, the analysis of user requirements may indicate that the demand can be met by enhancing current services. The next step is to obtain detailed information on the current usage patterns and volumes. With this information, it will be possible to formulate maximum, minimum and probable values for the proposed new usage. These data will form the basis for an outline capacity plan - see the **Capacity Management** module for further details.

Accurate figures on current usage can be obtained through the use of such network monitoring tools as response time monitoring systems and protocol monitoring systems for data networks, and call logging systems for voice networks.

Previous invoices for the use of external network services are also useful as an indication of volumes and costs.

For new networks, visits to similar installations can allow performance estimates to be made for the basic traffic patterns and data volumes.

Predict future traffic — Once the basic traffic patterns and volume data are obtained, they can be used as the basis for predicting future traffic levels. Account must be taken of differences between current and proposed usage. This must include the effects of changes in staff levels, relocations and other organizational changes together with predicted changes due to new technology such as desktop video conferencing.

Produce sizing estimate — From the basic traffic patterns, volume data and performance requirements, a sizing estimate can be produced. This estimate must include growth projections and contingency requirements. This type of sizing exercise is best done using modelling tools as they allow 'what-if?' analysis to be carried out quickly (see section 7 and annex E for further information on tools).

G.6 Prepare and validate statement of requirements

The outcome of the initial sizing exercise allows the project team to prepare a formal statement of requirements (SOR). The SOR must identify the business need being satisfied with each function or facility identified and the business benefits associated with them.

The SOR should then be validated by users to ensure that it meets their requirements. An important step in validating the SOR is to give a formal presentation of how the data and associated assumptions were obtained and used to project the final values. This allows users to understand fully the derivation of the data and challenge any erroneous assumptions made by the project team. If the SOR is accepted the project team can proceed to the design stage with confidence.

If the SOR is not given approval, the requirements must be reviewed in order to meet the objectives. This may require a re-definition of requirements or a change in the allocated budget.

Whilst all this takes time, the process must occur to ensure that:

* all parties involved in the project understand what functionality is proposed
* why this functionality is being proposed
* the proposed levels of service
* the resources required to support it are understood.

This exercise may be iterative to take account of multiple network services if the project is addressing more than one requirement. Each separate network service should be considered individually for business benefit in order that each service may be assessed independently.

G.7 Conduct initial costing exercise

Once the user requirements analysis and outline sizing exercises are complete, an overall cost of the functional requirements must be developed for each network service. This will reflect the full scope of the project. Each function or facility required by users or for management purposes must be clearly identified, prioritized and costed.

It can be useful to allocate an initial cost based on typical industry values to each function and facility. This cost can be on a per-user basis or a per-system or service basis depending on how it affects the overall costs of the service. The accuracy of these values is not significant, (within a margin of say 15%), if a consistent approach is taken to all aspects of the costing.

The costs derived are not an accurate estimate of the final costs of the project. The final costs depend on the design and implementation chosen. Nevertheless, it is important to obtain an estimate of the costs involved to allow a decision to be made as to whether to proceed with the project to the design stage.

It is important to consider the business benefits of each function and quantify any cost savings. A cost benefit analysis may be required to obtain an estimate of the final net value of each function and facility provided.

From the results of this costing exercise, the project team can prepare a detailed cost analysis and benefit profile for the project. This will enable business managers to evaluate the business worth of the proposed network service(s).

G.8 Project plan

A project plan must be produced and submitted for senior management (eg PRINCE Project Board) approval. The plan will contain:

* what needs to be done

* an estimate of the time-scales, skill levels and budget required for the remainder of the project

* the provisional cost model

* the provisional cost benefit analysis

* the results of the sizing exercise(s).

The material in the plan must be sufficiently detailed to allow decisions to be made on which aspects of the project should proceed to the design phase.

G.9 Design network

The design process attempts to match the user requirements with the available technology and resource limitations as effectively and efficiently as possible. This match must be achieved while taking into account the issues of cost and the 'life cycle' (ie from implementation until de-commission) requirements of on-going network services management and support.

The end result must be cost-effective. Achieving this requires a structured approach to the design process in both the task and its documentation.

It must be appreciated that network design is somewhat of a 'black art', that is highly dependent on the skills of the design team, and that, unless the network is very simple, it is not possible to evaluate all potential options. The best that can be achieved is to produce a draft design and cost it, then introduce a number of modifications to the design and see if any are cheaper and/or more effective. If they are, then incorporate these changes into the design as a basis for further modifications.

As the first step, it is important to derive from the statement of requirements (SOR) the basic functionality in technical terms. This will allow the technological requirements and range of viable options to be identified. These include, for example:

* centralized data systems - the networking of a mainframe host and terminals

Annex G
Planning and implementing network services

* de-centralized system, using local data network - the networking of microcomputers, LAN-LAN, LAN Internets or LAN-Host based services

* voice systems - a PABX or networked key systems

* wide area data networks - an shared (X.25) or dedicated (leased line) network

or combinations of all of these.

Constraints may already exist due to:

* the characteristics of the applications software or of supporting systems that are part of live IT services

* the organization's policies or in-house standards.

This may lead to overall designs that are less than optimum, but nevertheless are practical and cost-effective in the medium term.

The design decisions must be based on the core requirements and the traffic volumes associated with them. In most cases, there will not be a 'best' solution and several ways of meeting the requirements will be possible. Each potential design must be evaluated in terms of meeting business requirements and costs.

A wide range of skills and expertise are necessary to achieve an effective and practical solution; such skills and expertise are outside the scope of this module. Designers must be aware of the danger of being led by the technology of the latest network system or service.

An effective way of saving resources on network design (and on subsequent re-design and management) is to carry out a reference site visit. See annex D for further details of this process.

Designers should call on the expertise of others to gauge the impact of design decisions on the overall network service and related IT functions. This will involve consulting with specialists from, for example, Computer Operations, (both at application & systems level) MLPT, Capacity and Availability Management.

More strategic issues, such as moving to an integrated private network, may also have a major impact on the network service design. In the next section some of the basic issues for voice and data network design are highlighted. Each area is specialized and presents its own business and technical concerns.

G.9.1 Network design issues

Network design is driven by a number of factors, where cost is an important but not the predominate issue.

G.9.1.1 Business constraints

The design of the network will inevitably be constrained by characteristics of the Information Systems owned by the business it is supporting. For example, it may be necessary to implement two separate LANs in a single floor of a building in order to meet the performance required by a small number of users in a cost-effective manner. The use of a router or intelligent bridge between the two LANs could provide the required connectivity without subjecting all users to a common (lower) level of performance.

G.9.1.2 Topology

A principal design issue is topology, that is how combinations of the following components are used to build the required network:

* backbone networks
* voice networks
* LANs
* WANs
* MANs
* ISDN (for integrating voice and data traffic)
* network gateways, bridges and routers
* links
* third party networks (PTTs and VANs)
* network servers and services (eg E-mail and fax).

The advantages and disadvantages of each topology, from the point of view of:

* availability
* capacity/performance (amount of data & response time required)
* cost
* security
* availability of effective network management tools.

Annex G
Planning and implementing network services

must be taken into account in the design of the overall network and of each logical part of the network.

Availability

When considering availability, options are:

* for network links and services

    - multiple routes
    - alternate routes
    - use of public networks
    - use of alternate network suppliers (BT, Mercury, etc)
    - triangulated systems

* for network components

    - dial back-up units/modems for leased lines
    - use of digital services such as ISDN for on-demand bandwidth or back-up
    - duplicate systems
    - 'hot standby' systems
    - redundant units and power supplies
    - fall back configurations
    - fault tolerant systems
    - use of mirroring techniques and systems
    - use of duplexing techniques
    - use of error correcting code memory systems
    - use of redundant array of inexpensive discs (RAID) systems and architecture
    - use of uninterruptible power supplies (UPS) and generators
    - use of 'hot card' swap systems
    - use of on-site spares holding
    - identification of potential hire sources
    - committed supply arrangements with preferred suppliers.

Further discussion of technical design issues is outside the scope of this module. However, the **Specification and Management of a Cable Infrastructure** module covers many of them and there are many books and training courses available on the subject of network design - see Bibliography in section 8.

G.9.1.3 Digital versus analogue

The choice between digital and analogue transmission is, for equivalent transmission rates (inclusive of error handling), a low-level issue, although any costings should include the cost of extra equipment (such as modems) for analogue lines, and (possibly) new equipment for digital lines. However, digital links are gradually replacing analogue links because they can offer up to 100 times the speed of analogue links, and are inherently more reliable over long distances.

G.9.1.4 Intelligent components

Many network infrastructure components have significant processing and storage capability inherent in their architecture. In many cases this processing capacity enables the system to exhibit 'intelligent' behaviour. An example of this is the ability of a group of multiplexors to analyse and localize the cause of a network failure and then derive the best overall re-routeing strategy(ies) to restore service.

The design team must evaluate the use and advantages of intelligent network components. Other examples include:

* devices for interconnecting networks such as intelligent bridges, routers for LAN integration providing automatic best path routing, dynamic alternate routing protocol and address filtering

* devices which optimize the transmission of mixed traffic such as mixed multiplexer systems to carry voice and data with priority switching of voice and statistical multiplexing of data on the same link

* intelligent cluster controllers providing screen handling facilities for terminals.

These components ease the day-to-day control of the network but increase the need for effective administration and planning.

G.9.1.5 Data network options

There are a number of component links and services which may be used for all or part of the network. Examples are:

* the public switched telephone network (PSTN) - for data transmission, possible transfer bit rates up to 19.2Kbit/s with data throughput of approximately 60Kbit/s using compression techniques

* localized geographical connections using media such as twisted pair for connection, giving transport rates up to 64Kbit/s - typically used internally in buildings or between buildings that are collocated

* localized geographical connections using higher order media such as coaxial or optical fibre for connection, giving transport rates up to 100+Mbit/s - typically used internally in buildings or between buildings that are collocated

* point-to-point radio, microwave, infra-red, tropospheric scatter or satellite connection where connection by cable is not possible or economic

* local area networks such as
    - Ethernet
    - IBM Token Ring
    - Fibre Distributed Data Interface (FDDI)

* packet switched services such as BT's Global Network Service (GNS) - includes an X25 based service. Typical transfer rates up to 64Kbit/s, theoretical maximum 2Mbit/sec

* fast packet services such as
    - Frame Relay - typical transfer rates 2Mbit/sec, maximum 45Mbit/sec
    - BT's Switched Multi-megabit Data Service (SMDS), based on ATM (Asynchronous Transfer Mode) technology and offering 2, 4, 10, 16 or 25 Mbit/s transmission speeds

* simple leased analogue lines using modems. Possible transfer rates up to 19.2Kbit/s with data throughput of approximately 60Kbit/s using compression techniques

The IT Infrastructure Library
Network Services Management

* BT's Kilostream digital leased line services with 19.2Kbit/s or Kilostream N giving multiples of 64Kbit/s throughput (service is provided by one or more channels, but this is transparent to the service user)

* BT's Megastream digital leased line services of 2Mbit/s or 8Mbit/s or greater are possible

* Government Data Network (GDN), for UK Government users only.

A recent development is the Metropolitan Area Network. This uses high speed links (normally private lines, for cost reasons), to give the functionality of a local network (such as Ethernet) over a wider area. This could be useful for an organization whose offices are spread around a city but require the increased functionality of a LAN. There is, of course, no fundamental reason why LAN functionality should not be made available over any distance, but the cost is usually prohibitive.

Further information on data network services may be found in annex H.

G.9.1.6 Choice of mechanism

The choice of components is determined by a number of factors:

* diversity of connections required, eg point-to-point or one to many

* throughput required

* variability of locations, fixed or moving

* the need to connect to other organizations

* resilience of the connection

* security of connection

* the number of simultaneous connections required from each point

* the type and format of data being sent; binary file, unformatted text, formatted text (E-mail), still or moving image etc

* the period over which the connection is required

* the direction of flow of the data, eg one-way broadcast

* the cost of the mechanism.

G.9.1.7 Voice network options

Each transport mechanism has its own functional and economic characteristics that may or may not meet the connection requirements. These issues must be fully considered during the design process.

Voice network services design is inherently more straightforward than data services, largely because:

* transmission errors are not so critical as with data networks

* voice requires real-time transmission and so choices of transmission media are limited.

The core criterion for designing and developing a voice network strategy is cost for a basic voice service. This is because the economic break-even points for deciding on whether to develop a private voice network service, rather than utilize a public service, are relatively well defined.

There are a number of component links and services which may be used to for all or part of a voice network. Examples are:

* the public switched telephone network (PSTN)

* private networks, using Private Branch Exchanges (PBX) and/or Private Automated Branch Exchanges (PABX)

* leased lines

* Integrated Services Digital Networks (ISDN)

* Government Telecommunications Network (GTN), for UK Government users only

* Value Added Networks

* Virtual Private Networks such as BT's FeatureNet.

Note that much of the additional functionality that PABXs can offer such as 'Call Back When Free', 'Call Transfer' and 'Call Waiting' can increasingly be provided by public service systems. The increased availability of more function rich public services (such as the Centrex service and Virtual Private Networks (VPN)) only serve to decrease the functional differences between public and private service offerings.

This decreasing functional differentiation increases the complexity of the cost comparison as the costs of providing a private network over the life of the system need to be compared to the public network costs. This includes the cost of:

* core components, such as P(A)BXs, multiplexors and circuits
* support staff and equipment
* planning, administration and management
* growth in number of users and traffic.

Integrated networking strategies that use a common highway for voice and data traffic can increase the complexity of this calculation. However, each area must be treated separately, because the business benefits may be different, and similar criteria apply to both areas.

There are a number of specialist voice application services now available and these require more detailed consideration. These and other new technologies/standards may require expertise outside that of the network design team and yet their impact on the network design is fundamental. Further discussion of these areas is provided in annex I.

G.9.1.8 Security

The logical and physical security of the network must also be quantified. Security is of particular importance for communications networks because of the physical distribution - networks are the most vulnerable parts of IT systems.

When designing connections to an existing network or stand-alone system, it should be borne in mind that the security of the existing network may have to be improved in order to meet the requirements of the new or enhanced network.

Detailed guidance about security is available to UK government customers in **CCTA's IT Security Library**. Guide **C4** of the **CCTA Information Systems Guides** is available to all organizations for a precis of the relevant information.

CRAMM

The CCTA Risk Analysis and Management Method (CRAMM) inter alia, describes a means of identifying justifiable countermeasures to protect the confidentiality, integrity and availability of IT systems.

List the threats to the network and propose and cost out required counter-measures. To quantify resilience, order the network links by importance and then build resilience in for the most important links by risk and impact analysis.

G.9.2 Network modelling and simulation

See section 7 for information on network modelling and simulation.

G.10 Alternative solutions

For each design proposal, alternative solutions must be properly considered, ie this question must be answered:

'Are there better or more cost effective ways of achieving the same business aims using new or different technology and services?'.

Advantages may be obtained by, for example, using distributed rather than centralized processing, or a public service such as ISDN, or Managed Network Services (such as the GDN for government departments) or Value Added Network Services.

G.11 Integration with existing systems

For each potential design, consider whether existing systems and services can advantageously be integrated with the proposed new systems and services. However, this can occur only if the following criteria are met:

* the existing technology is considered adequate, eg in terms of functionality, performance and reliability (ie is able to meet Mean Time Between Failures and Mean Time To Recover levels)

* the integration can be done on a cost effective basis over a period (eg 2-3 years)

* the integration can be done without adversely affecting the existing service levels and either improve the functionality, performance, or availability at no net additional cost, or produce overall cost savings.

G.12 Costs

Typical costs and performance information for the base technologies chosen for each potential design can be obtained from suppliers. From this a complete cost analysis for each design should be carried out. Estimates should be made, either on a per-user basis or for the system as a whole. In some cases it may be necessary to include variable costs where, for example, scale of use has an effect on the cost structure.

This cost analysis provides the project team, and hence the users, with a guide to the costs associated with each aspect of the SOR. This is essential if the projected costs exceed the currently allocated budget. The information can be compared with the users' priority for each function to best match the design with the budget constraints of the project.

G.13 Evaluation of options

The result of considering various design options should be a range of design solutions, each with its advantages and disadvantages. A final comparative evaluation must then be carried out based on the business and user requirements, the cost profiles and the technical issues involved.

In carrying out the evaluation, it is essential to consider the operational and support issues such as:

* the required skill levels for network services staff

* the maintenance, support and training costs over the period of the plan (say 3 years)

* the costs of new test equipment for network support and projected hardware maintenance costs.

The design of the network topology must be clearly shown to conform to the capacity, availability, contingency and security requirements.

In a number of cases, it may be difficult to decide upon a single solution because of unknown variables. In these cases, refine each solution by modelling or simulating the criteria concerned and use comparative analysis techniques on the results.

G.14 Finalize design

Having analysed the costs, considered options and integration with existing systems, it is now possible to finalize the design, which provides the required functionality, for the period of the plan. The design must be based on the following considerations:

* support users' requirements for service levels; ie performance, reliability and availability (including resilience to faults)

* allow for the monitoring of service levels

* capacity - facilitate enhancements to accommodate projected growth in use of services and for projected new services

* contingency - provide for alternative facilities to be made available if any part of the network suffers prolonged failure

* meet all regulatory requirements

* be supportable by network services staff

* facilitate the provision of required support for vendors and maintainers

* facilitate the provision of customer support via Help Desk/Problem Management staff.

The maturity of the technology (ie how well proven it is) and the reliability of the suppliers must be taken into account. Where possible, a formal reference site visit should be arranged, to talk to other users of the proposed technology and customers of the potential suppliers. Guide-lines for carrying out a reference site visit are given in annex D.

G.15 Plan network implementation /enhancement

Once a final design has been selected, the implementation must be planned in detail.

The distributed nature of telecommunication networks makes the task of project managing implementations or enhancements very demanding. The implementation project team needs to be organizationally separate from the operational staff to ensure that:

* the current operational workload does not interfere with implementation work

* the implementation project is properly managed; this requires skills which may not be fully developed in the operational team

* there is a defined end-date by which the project must be completely finished and signed off

* separate teams exist to allow independent quality reviews to be undertaken.

The implementation project manager must liaise with other areas affected by implementation, such as staff from Computer Operations Management ie systems /applications programmers and Management of Local

Processors and Terminals, using the normal change management procedures (see the **Change Management** module). The manager of the implementation project must also maintain regular contact with any third party suppliers involved in the project. Hold regular meetings throughout the implementation period with service suppliers, hardware/software vendors, as well as with contracted staff ie installers or consultants. The communication procedure should be agreed prior to the implementation phase and should form part of any contract - see the **Managing Supplier Relationships** module for further details.

Coordination between the design team, the implementation team and network services operations staff is essential for this exercise.

In the case of a greenfield site, it is particularly desirable for the designers also to plan the operational support and managerial structures, methods and procedures that are required - see section 3 of this module for details.

Plan order of implementation	The order in which the implementation should be undertaken, if this is significant, should be specified.
Define implementation procedures	Practices and procedures must be defined before the implementation of new systems to ensure existing services are not interrupted. These practices and procedures must cover:

* site control, who can have access, where and when

* control of access to the live configuration, any changes, particularly those which may be discernible to end users, must be carefully controlled by the change management procedures

* installation and control of power and environmental systems

* liaison between implementation and operational teams

* cut-over and hand-over procedures, which have been reviewed and agreed by network operations in advance

* roll-back and roll-forward procedures, which have been defined, reviewed and agreed

* procedures to generate and review operational documentation

* procedures for system and service release control

Annex G
Planning and implementing network services

* version, build, inventory and configuration control procedures

* version and release control, via a defined creation and control procedure, for all documentation.

The activities to which these procedures apply affect operational staff both during and after the implementation work has been completed. It is therefore advisable for operational staff to check at this stage that the procedures are satisfactory and, later, that the activities are completed satisfactorily.

In the case of a network services enhancement, Network Services Control must have the final say about whether and when any aspect of the live network can be changed. Network Services Control is the configuration control authority for the network. In the case of a new installation Network Services Control has the final authority to accept or reject any aspect of the installed systems and services at the hand-over period.

The Bring Into Service (BIS) procedures detail the order in which systems and services become live and how the cut-over to live working takes place. The BIS procedures also identify relevant documentation about the installed systems and services that must be presented to the operations team.

This documentation forms a permanent record of what was installed, and of where and how it is configured. The documentation forms the basis of all the operational records for maintenance purposes. It must include:

* build and configuration information

* results journals for all tests carried out

* cut-over details and test traffic generation results

* back-out procedures

* roll-forward procedures, if no feasible back-out is possible

* a complete inventory of all systems, software and services, including all serial, model and version numbers, including installation details

* details of all warranty, maintenance and support for the systems and services

* all relevant geographical information, eg site plans, floor plans, room plans, rack layouts

- vendor details, including addresses, contact names, telephone numbers
- a complete set of all system and service documentation
- connectivity management details including cross-connect frame details, cable and wiring plans and equipment connection details
- a complete set of all invoices and other financial information connected with the project
- a complete set of all contracts and other agreements which form part of the project
- a complete set of user guides.

This information may be held in a number of different areas, for example:

- test traffic generation details may be held in the Capacity Management Database (CDB), see the **Capacity Management** module
- build and configuration details may form part of the Configuration Management Database (CMDB), see the **Configuration Management** module
- system and server documentation may form part of the Technical Network Library.

This should be decided prior to the implementation phase in order that the information is collected and then correlated in the correct format.

Plan configuration

Initial build and configuration information should be prepared for the network systems and circuits, for example:

- line speeds
- packet sizes
- routeing details
- error detection/correction parameters
- buffer sizes.

The build documentation for new systems and services must be thoroughly checked by Network Services Control before implementation commences. This is to ensure the build does not conflict with the provision of existing services. It also allows a final check that the new systems and services are operable and supportable.

Annex G
Planning and implementing network services

Capture existing configuration details	During implementation, an unrepeatable opportunity exists to obtain all the relevant data (unless it is already well documented and managed) concerning:

* equipment types, quantities and serial numbers, locations and users - see the **Configuration Management** module for further details

* equipment (including software) set-up procedures and parameters

* test and performance results, for regression tests

* financial and supplier details, see the **Configuration Management** and **Cost Management** modules for further details.

To take advantage of this opportunity, the necessary activities to collect, organize and document the information must be included in the project plan.

Plan to label equipment	Plan to label hardware and cables. The type of labelling system and its possible linkage to management packages such as that of a cable management system (see the **Specification and Management of a Cable Infrastructure** module for further information) or to a database system should also be planned for.
Plan to test contingency plans	The contingency plans should be tested during the implementation period to uncover any inadequacies or deficiencies that may exist within them. It is important to have a high degree of confidence in the effectiveness of the contingency plans as their failure can have a significant business impact. See the **Contingency Planning** module for further details.
Plan training	Plan for the provision of initial user training and establishing customer liaison procedures. Further information on customer liaison is available in the IT Infrastructure Library **Customer Liaison** module. Training for network control staff must be included.

Ensure that all staff have their training needs assessed and matched against any likely impacts and demands placed upon them from the installation of the new system. This training may take differing forms:

* network design and implementation team staff may require training in specific technologies

* training of members of Network Services Control may be completed prior to and during implementation

The IT Infrastructure Library
Network Services Management

* customer support ie Help Desk training/appreciation of new services, may be completed prior to and during implementation or may form part of an existing cross-training procedure

* the project team should highlight, at an early stage, the likely impact on users of the new network services and organize appropriate training and/or procedure changes.

Plan coordination with testing and computer installation staff	Coordination may be required with testing and computer installation staff if rolling out a new service or system. See the **Testing an IT Service for Operational Use** and **Computer Installation and Acceptance** modules for more details of these functions.
Plan hand-over	The hand-over period should be planned to start between 2 and 8 weeks before the Bring into Service (BIS) date and extends to 2 to 8 weeks beyond it, depending on the size of the project.

The responsibility for the network is transferred, during the hand-over period, from the implementation staff to the operations team. This transfer must be carefully controlled and signed off to ensure that the operational team take ownership of the network during the overlapping period.

An audit mechanism, to independently check the information being provided by the implementation team, must be agreed before the work starts. This ensures the quality of the information being provided and allows the operations team, who subsequently rely on it, to have confidence in it.

Testing and conformance reviews are required to determine the viability of the network for carrying traffic. However, testing alone cannot accurately simulate all aspects of how the installed systems are to be used. The network is fully tested only when the systems are made live. For this reason the hand-over period must span the BIS date for the network.

Implementation staff must be available to assist the operational staff in incident control and problem determination and resolution (ie Problem Management and Help Desk) during this period - eg to help Network Services Control to decide whether a failure is due to a system fault, a failure to meet the initial specifications or a misunderstanding or misuse by network operations or end-users.

Annex G
Planning and implementing network services

Further information on these subjects is available in the **Testing an IT Service for Operational Use** and **Configuration Management** modules.

Ensure that Network Services Control, Computer Operations Management, the Help Desk and Network Services Administration are informed in advance of the new system's introduction and that their processes and activities are amended accordingly before the BIS date.

Implementation staff should also be available to familiarize the operational staff with:

* preventative and corrective maintenance routines and the use of test equipment

* restart, reload and re-configuration procedures

* the scope of control available of equipment distributed across the network eg whether diagnostics can be initiated and produced at the central site or must be carried out at the remote site.

Plan acceptance tests

The implementation team is responsible for demonstrating, to the satisfaction of Network Services Control, that the installed systems and services conform to the planned specifications. This should be achieved through a rigorous set of acceptance test specifications which are agreed in advance of the implementation work starting. The development of these test specifications is the responsibility of the planning team and an independent test team; the network service designers will be able to provide valuable input, however, on the completeness of the test specifications.

The tests required depend upon the size and critical nature of the network in question. In the case of a large or a critical network it is advisable to create a test environment for systems and services to allow pseudo-live testing before bringing them into service. The use of traffic generators to do both local and end-to-end tests, enabling live checks during non-critical periods, for example at night, is recommended.

The acceptance test plans must cover all aspects of the systems and services involved in the project and include:

* functional test specifications - these specifications must test the functionality of the network and address, for example, the following questions

    - does the network react as expected to spurious inputs?

G23

- does the network accept and react correctly to inputs from protocol generators?
- do the auto-reroute mechanisms function as expected?

* performance test specifications - these specifications define tests on the performance of the network, and address, for example, the following questions

  - is the terminal response time equal to the expected sum of all the components' store and forward and/or response times?
  - under various simulated load conditions, do response times meet requirements?

* some form of load testing to simulate the effects of the expected typical traffic levels. This can be achieved by using voice and data traffic generators.

The implementation team must be able to demonstrate clearly the conformance of the systems and services to the test specifications. The operations team must sign off this conformance at each test phase. A phased test acceptance document signed by both parties is often used for this purpose.

From the viewpoint of the operational staff, the fundamental question which needs to be answered at the hand-over point of a service is: 'Is it ALL documented, does it meet the specification, does it work to the satisfaction of the users and is it manageable?'

In particular, the operations staff must:

* be satisfied with the extent of the tests being carried out ie that the functionality being tested is comprehensive

* understand the confidence levels associated with the test specifications. It is not always possible to test every conceivable aspect of the systems and services involved. However, it is important to know what limits for potential errors or oversight exist in the test strategy

* understand the accuracy and reliability of results generated.

Plan for auditing of tests | Insist on some form of 'Test Log and Journal' approach to testing. This allows subsequent auditing of the tests carried out and ensures that the results obtained are consistent and as documented.

Annex G
Planning and implementing network services

	Plan to perform both regular and impromptu audit reviews of the testing work being done by the installation team. This ensures procedures are being adhered to and quality standards met.
Plan for re-testing	Establish a coherent policy and supporting procedures to re-test systems and services which fail initial testing. The level and scope of re-testing must be carefully considered to ensure that the extent of any failures are fully investigated and resolved.
Plan integration tests	Following the installation of the network, a series of Integration Tests must also be carried out. These tests prove the inter-working of all the discrete elements (such as the network and servers attached to it) installed and independently tested.
	Coordination between acceptance tests for networks, computer systems and the overall IT service may be required - see the IT Infrastructure Library modules on **Testing an IT Service for Operational Use** and **Computer Installation and Acceptance** for more guidance on this subject.
Plan for roll-back	It is good practice to run the old and new systems in parallel for a period; if however this is not possible, or even if it is possible, a plan must be prepared to deal with the new system failing. This must take account of how long it would take to recover or replace the failed elements and restore service, or to revert to the old system (if this is feasible).
Discuss plan	A successful relationship between the implementation and operations teams is necessary for the success of any IT project. For this to occur, the implementation plan must be agreed with the operational and implementation teams well in advance of the intended activities.

Annex H. Data network services

This annex outlines some of options available for data network services.

Electronic mail

Electronic mail (E-Mail) facilities may be provided either in-house or by commercial hosts such as Apple Link, Telecom Gold, Telemail, or Mercury LINK 7500. Concerns may be raised over:

* menus
* international interconnection
* response times
* availability
* gateways
* billing
* terminal emulation
* distribution lists.

Message handling systems

Message handling systems (MHS) - these enable the exchange of electronic messages between different systems using a common approach. Concerns may be:

* addressing messages
* storage of messages
* submission of messages
* delivery of messages
* message routeing and transportation.

The ITU/TSs X.400 standard has been commercially adopted and most of the above concerns have now been addressed.

Electronic data interchange

Electronic data interchange (EDI) - provides a mechanism for the transfer of structured data from computer to computer with a publicly agreed format and meaning. When used for commercial data this technology is often known as paper-less trading.

Groups in various commercial sectors such as banking, aerospace and insurance have formed user groups to encourage the use of and benefit from the cost savings, administration improvements, reduced time delays in trading operations and improvements in cash flow that EDI offers.

Concerns for the design team are:

* hardware & software costs
* research and project management costs
* training
* communication link types
* existing standards such as ODETTE, TRADACOMS, EDIFACT.

Emerging technologies and systems also need to be considered and may require evaluation or even pilot testing.

Integrated Services Digital Networks

Integrated Services Digital Networks (ISDN) provide for switchable digital access for voice and/or data to the customer's premises. Considerations include:

* connection and usage costs
* ISDN access availability
* level of access available
* system interfaces available, ie for PCs, fax, PABX, LANs etc
* broadband ISDN.

The perceived business benefit is the higher throughput possible on a switched basis.

ISDN can be considered as a digital variant of the existing public telephone service.

Fibre Distributed Data Interface

Fibre Distributed Data Interface (FDDI) is a high speed fibre optic transport mechanism for interconnection of lower speed LANs or high speed devices. It is particularly immune to electromagnetic interference. Considerations include:

* costs
* bridge access
* security
* Twisted Pair Distributed Data Interface (TPDDI) - use of the FDDI protocol over the cheaper, twisted pair medium for distances up to about 100 metres.

Broadcast technology

The emergence of Very Small Aperture Terminals (VSATs) and the licensing of six Special Satellite Service Operators (SSSOs) for the transmission of signals represents a new area of network service offerings in Europe.

Typical applications in this area include the retail sector, where the use of broadcast technology may be useful to bulk update many sites with information such as new price lists for inventory items.

Annex I. Voice network services

This annex outlines some of the options available for voice network services.

There is an increasing number of specialist voice based applications available. This has been driven by the increased processing capability becoming available at low cost and the greatly reduced cost and increased capacity of Winchester disk storage (1Gbyte disks are not expensive).

It is anticipated that many new voice based system offerings will become available on a range of platforms from the PC through to large scale integrated computer and digital switching systems. A number of manufacturers, for example DEC and IBM, already offer the first generation of such systems.

The specialist applications may include:

* voice messaging (Voice Mail) - computer recording of messages in electronic mailboxes for remote or local retrieval

* automatic call distribution (ACD) - automated call assistance, queuing and distribution

* audiotex - the retrieval of information in recorded voice or fax format. More sophisticated versions use digital tone multi-frequency (DTMF) tones to obtain recorded information

* voice response - enables DTMF phone users to use the key pad to establish a link and enables (eg) a password to be entered to gain access to financial information

* integrated voice and switch processing co-ordinated with computer based application services

* voice recognition systems, to provide an automated but friendly service to callers - expected to replace or augment voice response technology.

These systems may be used for:

* call diversion to mailboxes

* call diversion to portable phones

* daily team briefings

* fax reception, storage and retrieval

* handling credit enquiries for dial-up retail or banking services.

These may also be integrated with other processing facilities to provide even more specialized business services.

IT Infrastructure Library
Network Services Management

Comments Sheet

CCTA hopes that you find this book both useful and interesting. We will welcome your comments and suggestions for improving it.
Please use this form or a photocopy, and continue on a further sheet if needed.

From:

        Name

        Organisation

        Address

        Telephone

COVERAGE
Does the material cover your needs?
If not, then what additional material would you like included?

CLARITY
Are there any points which are unclear?
If yes, please detail where and why.

ACCURACY
Please give details of any inaccuracies found.

If more space is required for these or other comments. please continue overleaf

IT Infrastructure Library
Network Services Management

Comments Sheet

OTHER COMMENTS

Information Systems Engineering Group
CCTA
Rosebery Court
St Andrews Business Park
Norwich, NR7 0HS

Further information

Further information on the contents of this module can be obtained from:

Information Systems Engineering Group
CCTA
Rosebery Court
St Andrews Business Park
NORWICH
NR7 0HS

Telephone 01603 704704
(GTN: 3040 4704)